To Kathy —
Congratulations! You
touch the Future —
        Sincerely
        Grace Corrigan
        July 24, 2005

Grace George Corrigan

A Journal for Christa

Christa McAuliffe, Teacher in Space

University of Nebraska Press
Lincoln and London

◎

First Bison Books printing: 2000
Most recent printing indicated
by the last digit below:
10 9 8 7 6 5 4 3 2 1
Library of Congress Cataloging-in-
Publication Data
Corrigan, Grace George, 1924–
A journal for Christa :
Christa McAuliffe, teacher in space/
by Grace George Corrigan.   p.   cm.
ISBN 0-8032-1459-6 (cl: alk. paper)
ISBN 0-8032-6411-9 (pa: alk. paper)
1. McAuliffe, Christa, 1948–1986.
2. Challenger (Spacecraft) – Accidents.
3. Teachers – New Hampshire – Biography.
4. Astronauts – United States – Biography.
I. Title. TL789.M33C67   1993
629.45'0092 – dc20   [B]   93-437 CIP

To Christa with love, Mom

A celebration
of Christa's life for
our children
and grandchildren

Contents

From July 19, 1985, to January 28, 1986, Christa was in the national eye. In that short time, she became teacher, daughter, sister, and friend to people all over the world, and, as such, her death affected each and every one.

Christa started writing a journal when she was pregnant with her first child, Scott. She wanted to communicate the experiences of a young mother to her child. She commented, "I would have loved it if my mother had said, 'Here, Christa, this is what my life was like.'"

I have, Christa.

Introduction

I wish that I could speak to you in Christa's voice, but I cannot. And I cannot even tell you that I know what she would have said, because Christa, like all of us, was special and was herself. I think, however, that I can tell you something about her, about her life, and about what she valued. I know that I can share with you the perspective of those closest to her: those who loved her and who were loved by her.

Through this journal, I hope to leave with you at least a suspicion that great people are really ordinary people who tried their best, who tried even though they might have been afraid to fail, and who, above all else, know the vital necessity for each of us to be true to ourselves.

Christa knew these things, and she acted on that knowledge. Our daughter is a hero, a real hero, but perhaps not for the reasons that you might think. She is not a hero because she died while seeking to expand her knowledge and to explore space. She is not a hero because she took a calculated risk as the first private citizen to venture into space. She is not a hero because she brought such needed credit to a great but beleaguered profession.

Rather, she is a hero because long before the Teacher-in-Space program was ever thought of, she overcame many of life's ordinary obstacles and became a worthy person, a person of value to herself and of value to those who shared this life with her. In short, she is a real hero because she actually did with her life what each of us is capable of doing with our own lives. Christa *lived*. She never sat back and just existed.

Christa always accomplished everything that she was capable of accomplishing. She extended her own limitations. She cared about her fellow human beings. She did the ordinary, but she did it well and unfailingly. And, as the media brought Christa before the nation, we all recognized in her what we like best in ourselves as a people – modesty, unselfishness, effort, exuberance, generosity, a sense of fun, and the ability to overcome fear.

Christa, like the rest of us, was human, with human worries and human frailties. She was normal – the girl next door. But unlike many of us, Christa worked, and worked unceasingly, to become the best person she could be. She suppressed her fears and conquered life's challenges – the real, everyday challenges that we have all faced and that we will continue to face. She placed others before herself. She placed personal honor above personal gain. She knew who she wanted to be, and she never stopped trying to become that person. She was not fearless anymore than you and I are fearless. But she wouldn't succumb to fear or weakness. Through determination and a clear vision of what is important, she refused to let any fear, especially the fear of failure, keep her from trying, from seizing the moment and extracting from each moment however much that life offered her.

The real heroes are people like Christa, people like parents and teachers who help children in ways they may never even realize. Real heroes are people who take everyday problems in stride and persevere without ever losing sight of who they are and of what is important.

Christa saw the year of her space experience as a grand and welcome opportunity for education – an opportunity to draw our attention in a positive way to schools, to our children, and to community involvement in improving our flagging educational system. This would be a year of awareness, a year to elevate the role of teachers to the height it should have. She knew that her colleagues would be judging her because she represented them. She regarded this as a tremendous responsibility, but she gladly accepted it because she was a committed teacher and felt that this shared experience would enhance the role of teachers, improve education, and inspire her students – those young people who are our future.

During the selection process, Teacher-in-Space nominees were required to provide a videotaped interview made under the direction of their local board of education. A question (not known in advance) asked the candidates to "describe your philosophy of living." Christa answered that her philosophy was first to get as much out of life as possible, to be flexible, to try new things, and to connect with people. A meaningful life needs some organization and involvement in community affairs, she said. She pointed out that one reason she went into teaching was to have an impact on others and to feel that impact on herself – she often said that she learned as much from her students as she taught them. She said that she felt a strong obligation to enjoy life, and certainly to involve others in that enjoyment.

The selection team felt they had what they were looking for when they viewed Christa's tape. And then she proved them right in Washington and Houston by going through all the final examinations and interviews with what NASA professionals called the "right stuff." It took the judges only twenty minutes to decide, and then they gave her all seven votes. Christa was going to fly!

A few news reporters tried to suggest that her primary goal was to make money, and that she planned to use the honor as a stepping stone to a career change. These skeptics seemed to know little about schools and the teaching profession, and Christa was exasperated by them. "Anything would be better than teaching," one reporter suggested. "All you have to do is be yourself – teaching is easy," said another. Christa patiently tried to convince them that teaching was an honorable, difficult, and essential profession. She not only said so privately, but she tried to make this perspective of teaching a matter of public record whenever she had the chance. She also made it a matter of record that she would indeed be back at Concord High School in the fall of 1986. "If the Teacher in Space does not return to the classroom," she said, "then something is wrong."

The space frontier, like the future, belongs to all of us. Christa wanted students and teachers to know that, to become involved, and to become excited. If she could do that, she felt, she would have done her job – both as a teacher and as the Teacher in Space.

Press conferences were regularly held by the *Challenger* crew at the Johnson Space Center in Houston. During one of the first press conferences, among visitors allowed in the press room was a group of students on a field trip. As the reporters finished with their questions, the students spontaneously began to come up to the stage to ask Christa questions. Christa saw these students listening carefully to her every word and asking excitedly about what space was like and what it would be like for them. She said that during that whole time she thought, "It's working – it's really working – this program is already working!" She took delight in participating in what she believed was a renewal of our national spirit.

Did Christa capture the heart of the nation? I hope so. Did she inspire us to live better lives? I hope that's true, too. Because Christa herself was inspired by teachers who taught her the importance of knowledge and values, by religious who taught her the importance of yearning to know who we are and why we exist, by family and friends who taught her about love and helping and sharing and fun, by forebears who taught her the precious value of freedom and adventure and nobility, and by poets and dreamers who taught her to dream and to strive to bring her dreams about. In turn, I hope that Christa's spirit will inspire you in some small way, too. (Adapted from Grace George Corrigan's Framingham State College commencement address, May 1986).

I

Countdown:
1985-86

A Card from Christa

One day in November 1985, a card was delivered postmarked Houston, Texas, and addressed only to me. It wasn't my birthday, so what was the occasion? I tore it open, read it, and let out a whoop of laughter; handing it to my husband, Ed, I said, "That Christa! Isn't she something?"

The card showed a snow scene and a jagged mountain peak with a cartoon of a climber reaching the top and setting a flag in the snow. With her left hand, she pulls the right hand of another climber whose nose, cap, and right mitten show over the mountain as she struggles to pull herself to the top.

The caption in the clouds above the picture reads, "Behind every great woman . . ."; when the card is opened, the caption continues, ". . . is another great woman." The picture inside shows the two women sitting together on top of the mountain. The first figure has her arm around the second figure and an unfurled flag reads, "Thanks, Mom!"

She signed it, "love, Christa" and wrote on the opposite page, "I saw this card in Dallas and just had to get it."

I attached the card to my refrigerator with a magnet, a homey place, easily seen. With great delight I would show it to everyone who came to our house.

Now I still show the card, but it is with a sense of sad togetherness. We two on top of the world!

Super Bowl Sunday

The *Challenger* liftoff with the added attraction of the Teacher-in-Space program had generated so much interest that it was difficult to get housing at Cape Canaveral unless advance reservations were made. Since we were responsible for our own housing at the Cape my husband and I had reserved a block of rooms at the EconoLodge so our family and friends who wanted to could be together. Ed and I needed space to entertain and celebrate, so from a list that Christa gave us, we contacted Cape Winds condominiums. We rented an apartment there large enough to sleep six, and invited Ed's brother Jim and his wife, Helen, and our friends Art and Nancy Marasco to share it with us. Our son Stephen and his wife, Anne, originally thought they wouldn't be able to make it, but when they arrived unexpectedly from California, the Cape Winds found them a room on another floor.

NASA canceled the flight scheduled for Sunday, January 26, 1986, because the weather was supposed to be bad. Ed and I opened our Cape Canaveral door early that morning to see a glorious sunny day and our son Stephen standing there huddled up in rain gear, his hood tied snugly under his chin, laughing: "NASA sure predicted this horrible wind and rainstorm. It's a good thing the flight was canceled!"

That afternoon, the New England Patriots were playing in their first Super Bowl game. Since the liftoff was canceled, we decided to throw a Super Bowl party and invited everyone we could reach. The function room in the Cape Winds was available for a party, and had a large television and plenty of space for a crowd. Everyone was psyched up.

Barbara Morgan, Christa's alternate, who was scheduled to provide the on-ground introductions for the space lessons, was using the nearby laundry room while visiting her in-laws at the Cape Winds. Hearing us all in the function room, she stopped by, laundry basket in hand, to say hello. Then, of course, so many wanted to meet her that it was quite a while before she was able to leave.

Since the flight had been canceled, reporters were looking for news anywhere they could. So many of them descended on us that Linda Long took over and set up a schedule. Linda was a public relations official who had been hired by NASA to help arrange Christa's appearances, interviews, and travel requirements. She allowed the reporters to come in one at a time with their crews. Each would set up cameras and lights and interview us. Then the newspeople went among our friends interviewing them while they were watching the game.

I thought that this was one of the best parties we had ever given. It was certainly different. Everyone was having a wonderful time. "Wait till I tell Christa all about it tonight!" I thought. "She has provided such fun for us all."

I quipped to one reporter, "It's beer for the Patriots today and champagne for Christa tomorrow."

The Patriots lost the game. Beers and cheers had not helped our team.

The champagne bottles never did get opened.

Liftoff

It was cold, cold, cold. Groups of people were awaiting liftoff huddled together, stamping their feet and wrapping their arms around themselves trying to keep warm. Others were bunched on the observation benches wrapped in borrowed blankets. The word was out that today was the day – definitely. Everyone wondered why a liftoff should be scheduled in such freezing weather. We could see icicles hanging from the shuttle. How could they lift off like this? But the night before, Christa told us they had been given a positive go-ahead for the morning. The *Challenger* launch had been postponed four times in all; two times previously we had gotten as far as the launch site. The first postponement was due to a dust storm in Africa, near the emergency landing site; the second was caused by a hatch bolt that couldn't be removed (at first the technicians couldn't find a screwdriver; when they did finally get one, it proved to have no batteries). Two other postponements were caused by bad weather, and the decisions were made before we went out to the site. The third time we reached the launch site was January 28, 1986.

At her last public appearance, Christa alighted from a NASA jet that flew the *Challenger* shuttle crew to Florida from their Houston base; "I'm so excited to be here," she said. "I don't think any teacher has been more ready to give two lessons. I hope everybody tunes in."

Among the personal items Christa had with her as she entered the shuttle were a Bob Dylan tape, a Girl Scout pin, her sister Betsy's Claddagh ring, her husband Steve's VMI class ring, her daughter Caroline's gold crucifix and chain (which Ed and I had given her at her baptism), and her son Scott's stuffed frog Fleegle. (Christa had told Scott that she might have to take out Fleegle's stuffing to make room for the frog in her pack; he was horrified. She quickly said not to worry; she would make sure it would fit.) She was also wearing her grandmother's diamond watch. Astronauts were given a certain amount of space to carry keepsakes for their friends and families.

Launch pad 39 B was being used for the first time. During the fall, the crew preparing the pad for this liftoff sent Christa a telegram to assure her that she should not be worried about the pad. It would be in perfect condition for the teacher! Perhaps it was, but the weather was not.

Looking out over the field at the shuttle *Challenger* sitting on the launch pad, we tried to picture the crew strapped into their seats waiting in anticipation for the countdown. Was Christa nervous? Probably not; just terribly excited. We knew that it was a long uncomfortable wait and that she had passed some of the time in previous delays by taking a nap.

"I'd take her off that thing if I could get out there," Ed said. We were getting edgy. Things didn't seem to be going the way we thought they should. "Even if you could, she wouldn't come," I answered.

The *New York Times* wanted to do an article about us watching the lift-off with the third-grade children from Scott's class, who had come down from New Hampshire to watch the launch. They asked if we would sit with the children in the VIP area, where reporters and photographers were able to see into the stands from behind the fenced-in area, instead of sitting in the family area which was off-limits to reporters. We agreed to sit with the class as long as it didn't create a problem. We were told to go ahead. Scott, however, wasn't with his classmates; he was with his father and sister and the spouses and children of the other crew members, watching the launch from a NASA building.

There was still quite a wait, so Ed and I visited with the Teacher-in-Space finalists, NASA personnel, and some of our friends. Christa had become very close to the other teacher candidates. Finally getting to meet the other finalists was a highlight of our trip. The bond among them was strong, and we felt as if we knew them all.

Then it was time to get settled on our bench. Dr. Robert Brown, director of NASA's Education Affairs Division, walked us over to the section where the children were sitting. Reporters and cameras were lined up behind the fence. Having met so many of them, we smiled and waved before turning to climb up to our seats.

Joining us in the VIP area were our children Christopher (Kit) and Lisa, Lisa's husband Bob Bristol, our brothers and their wives, and friends Nancy and Art Marasco. Christa's friend Jo Ann Jordan was chaperoning the schoolchildren, and when she saw us coming she moved down to sit with us.

Our other children had left for California during the night, unable to stay any longer. Our daughter Betsy and Angelica Ramos, her business partner and friend, had to reopen their delicatessen. Our son Stephen was scheduled to take his California law boards in a few days, and he and his wife, Anne, were anxious to get back to their children.

The huge digital clock had started its countdown. Unexpectedly, I was racked with sobs. Ed's arms tightened around me, and Lisa squeezed my hand.

Countdown. Liftoff. Cheers and then silence.

"She's gone," Ed said.

"But I can't see the shuttle!"

"Then she's really gone."

Below, Dr. Brown was slowly walking over to our section. Looking up, he sadly shook his head and beckoned for us to come down from the bleachers.

I said to Ed, "They were too complacent. How could they possibly take any kind of a chance with the lives of seven such beautiful people?" Was it easier for me to think of Christa as not being alone?

Ed looked at me. "But it's *your* daughter! Your firstborn! How you must be hurting. I'll miss her every day for the rest of my life."

Family and friends closed ranks around us as we walked out of the VIP area to the waiting buses.

Shirley McNearney from Boston's channel 4 watched us as we walked by. Just that Sunday morning we had given Shirley an interview outside the condominium. Her cameraman swung the camera around to focus on us, but Shirley put her hand over the lens.

When President Reagan heard the news he asked, "Is that the flight the teacher is on?" He canceled his State of the Union address scheduled for that evening.

On the six o'clock news from channel 5 Boston, Natalie Jacobson stopped showing the footage of the explosion that had been running all day and said, "It is time to give the families some privacy."

From the many letters we later received, one child's words could aptly be applied to what followed: "No one knows what to do, but they are working on it."

Those sitting in the family section had been taken into an auditorium. The doctors saw the deep anger in Ed's calmness. They were concerned about a heart attack and tried to give him medication. He refused. All we wanted was to see Steve and the children, and get some information – which no one had.

Years later, I was to find among my husband's papers several hand-written pieces about what he called "NASA's ineptitude." One page lists a dozen names of high-ranking NASA officials – decision makers – and

5

NASA's expert advisers, each of whom had advised against the launch. Ed wrote,

"I have been angry since January 28, 1986, the day Christa was killed. Being at the launch site in Florida where we could observe NASA's ineptitude first-hand certainly did nothing to bolster confidence in the Challenger launch.

The first day the launch was to be made, NASA canceled because of a sandstorm in Africa which might impede an emergency landing. It was a beautiful day in Florida – and warm. The next delay was on January 27 when all the king's horses and all the king's men couldn't get a screw out of a hatch on the Challenger. They finally located a battery-run screwdriver to fix it – but forgot the battery. Then they canceled because of cold temperatures. But the next day was equally cold or colder, and they attempted the launch.

My daughter Christa McAuliffe was not an astronaut – she did not die *for* NASA and the space program – she died *because of* NASA and its egos, marginal decisions, ignorance, and irresponsibility. NASA betrayed seven fine people who deserved to live. One of the Commissioners stated, "It was no accident; it was a mistake that was allowed to happen."

When Christa was in the Teacher-in-Space Program, we felt no great fear that she would be risking her life for a cause. I am sure that if anyone had advised her how flawed NASA management was, she would never have risked leaving her husband and children.

President Reagan said that the act was not deliberate, was not criminal. But I say that sins of omission are no less sins than those of commission. I say "they" deliberately neglected to make necessary corrections to the O-rings and are, therefore, as guilty as if they planned a deliberate criminal act . . .

People in our country and all over the world have given us great love and support, and we appreciate it.

My attitude, I am sure, differs from that of astronauts' spouses and families. I feel no allegiance to NASA."

Following the Launch

We found our son-in-law Steve McAuliffe and grandchildren Scott and Caroline in Christa's dormitory room at the Kennedy Operation and Checkout building. Christa had left there only that morning. Her sneakers were on the floor and her running suit was lying on top of her flight bag. Her name plate was on the door.

Steve's first words were, "This is not how it is supposed to be!" We tried to comfort each other. Then, after a while, he said to me, "But you grew up without a mother and you turned out all right."

We stood, we sat, we waited and waited and waited.

Steve's mother, Rita, came in and hugged the kids. After Rita, Steve's brother Wayne arrived, followed by our children Kit and Lisa, and Lisa's husband, Bob.

Lisa slipped Christa's NASA nameplate from the door and handed it to Scott. From his pocket Steve took out Teacher-in-Space pendants with chains. He handed them to Lisa. "Christa bought these; I was to give them to you after she had lifted off." Lisa said it made her feel as if she were six years old again, a time when her sister would often surprise her with unexpected gifts.

I worried about my other children, Betsy and Steve; they should have reached their homes in California by this time. Arrangements needed to be made. Barbara Morgan was in the large living area just waiting to help. Upset as Barbara was, she handled the calls, reaching Betsy as she came into her house from the Los Angeles airport. Since the family would all be going home to Framingham, outside Boston, Betsy picked up the luggage that she had just put down and headed back to the airport for a flight to San Francisco to travel home with Steve and Anne.

When Steve and Anne walked into their house, they turned on the television set to see if the liftoff was being broadcast. They found themselves watching the explosion. Their friends and neighbors gathered to help them unpack, repack, and get their boys ready to travel. Two-year-old David and three-year-old Brian were to come this time.

Plane reservations were made on a direct flight so there wouldn't be the hassle of changing planes. When Betsy came in from Los Angeles, they all left San Francisco together for Boston. But first, the plane touched down in Los Angeles, at the airport Betsy had left only hours before. In the hurry and confusion, no one thought of the difference between a direct flight and a nonstop flight!

Ed felt as if he were being held prisoner in Christa's room. We were not given any information except that the vice president was on his way. I kept going in and out of the room. I would see the other families. We'd hug, try to say something, or just exchange a look. Needing to be doing something, I brought back coffee, tea, and cold drinks that nobody wanted. We were all uneasy, trying to comfort one another, waiting without hope for any news. Caroline and Scott stayed close to their father, understanding yet not understanding. But did any of us really understand?

George Abby, flight crew operations director, came to the door, silently shook Steve's hand, and left.

Ed just could not stand to be in Christa's room any longer, so I tried to find someone to take us back to the Cape Winds. NASA officials tried to persuade us to stay, but I insisted we leave. After a delay we were given an escort to the highway, and from there the state police drove us to the condo.

Crowds were milling around the grounds. A path was made for us, and the police kept everyone back. We finally were able to close the door and be with our family and friends (although one enterprising reporter was able to get through the police barricade, climb up from the pool area, and land on the balcony).

Nancy Marasco recently asked me if I remembered what I said when I came into the apartment. I couldn't, so she reminded me: "She was doing what she wanted to do." I had and still have a mother's fierce desire to defend her young, although Christa's actions need no defending. She had led a full, exemplary life and died with exceptional companions at the moment of her dreams being fulfilled.

Ethel Corrigan, Ed's cousin, was trying to make some order out of the chaos. New travel arrangements were needed and places to stay had to be found for those who had given up their rooms but were now staying.

Back at Kennedy Center, the vice president had arrived. NASA called to ask us to come back, but we declined. Meanwhile, confusion reigned everywhere; Christa's friend Jo Ann Jordan struggled to help the confused and frightened children from Scott's class get back to their buses, and to shield them from the swarms of reporters. One reporter threw himself in front of the bus to stop it from leaving so his photographer could get some pictures.

That afternoon back home in Framingham, our friends had been seeing the explosion and our reaction replayed over and over on television. Ceil Wohler, who was looking after our dog, Jessie, once Kit left home to meet us in Florida, called our church from our house to ask Father

William O'Connor, our pastor, to have a Mass said. "Where have you been?" he replied. "I've been trying to reach you. The Cardinal is coming to Framingham to say Mass at seven o'clock tonight. We would like you and Charlie to bring the gifts of the people to the altar."

Later that evening, we answered a call from Framingham; it was Ceil, calling from the rectory of St. Jeremiah's. Would we take a call from Cardinal Bernard Law, Archbishop of Boston? His Eminence said that his prayers were with us and that an overflow crowd had just attended a Mass he celebrated in our church for Christa and all the astronauts. We also spoke to Father O'Connor. Father, a classmate of Ed's at Boston College, had been at our parish less than six months. He met Christa one Sunday after Mass and then commented on how well she handled herself. He noted that she made time for each one waiting to speak to her and carefully considered every question asked of her.

Ceil then came back on the line to report that she and Charlie were taking care of everything they could and that they would sleep over in our house that night, as they believed the house should be occupied. While they went to the memorial Mass, their children Mary Beth and Jim housesat.

Flags were at half-mast as we left Florida the next day. The Teacher-in-Space souvenir signs were replaced with condolences, as were other roadside signs we passed. Cars were being driven with their headlights on, and everything and everyone seemed so quiet. Airport security and airline personnel were wonderful. From the moment our cars entered the airport, we were met and driven to a private gate by the police. Delta employees then escorted us over the tarmac to where the plane was waiting.

Crowds were jammed on the covered catwalk, trying to see into the airplane. Reporters were buying tickets for the flight. No one was allowed to carry any cameras on board.

Our children Kit and Lisa were with us, as were Lisa's husband, Bob, and his sister Sally. Their mother, Gert Bristol, came to the plane to see us off and then had the lonely drive back to her home in Englewood in western Florida. So many of our relatives and friends had driven long distances and were now faced with a joyless ride home.

Ed and I had asked Linda Long if she could come home with us. Linda didn't hesitate, saying, "as long as you need me." When we reached Boston's Logan Airport, our baggage was collected, and to avoid the reporters we deplaned while the plane was still on the runway. We were told that some reporters had bought tickets just to be in the passenger gate area in the terminal.

We could see our son Stephen waiting, holding his son Brian on his shoulders. Father O'Connor was with him. State troopers from Massachusetts and New Hampshire were in unmarked cars to take our luggage and drive us home. Framingham police were waiting at our house, but even so reporters shoved cameras into our faces and blocked the entranceway into the house.

Betsy saw what was happening from the window, and quickly opened the garage door so some of us were able to dash in that way. We had been home only a few hours when the doorbell rang. A reporter from the *National Enquirer* was standing there when our son Steve opened the door. "We will give you $100,000 for an exclusive interview." Steve shut the door without bothering to answer.

We were grateful to Delta Airlines and the police for taking care of us and making a distressful trip as easy as it could possibly be. We were thankful to be home.

II

Early Years:
1940s-1960s

Our Family Begins

Ed and I were friends throughout high school, often double dating. After we graduated I went on to art school, and Ed went to college before joining the Navy in the early days of World War II. He served four years as a radioman, seeing action in both the Atlantic and Pacific theaters. Ed was honorably discharged in 1946 and that New Year's Eve invited me to a party. We were married in Waterbury, Connecticut on July 26, 1947, about a month before he was to start as a freshman at Boston College's School of Business Administration. Our families gave their blessings and advice: "You just might make it if you don't have any children." Four years later, on June 13, 1951, two-and-a-half-year-old Christa watched as her father received his degree, while two-and-a-half-month-old Kit stayed at home with a sitter.

When we arrived in Boston for Ed's freshman year, our first apartment was at 51 Park Drive on the fourth floor. The elevator worked only part-time. We had one room and a tiny kitchen, bath, and foyer. The first time we saw it, the apartment was filthy and needed painting. The windows looked out on the brick wall of the next apartment building about six feet away.

Many of Ed's friends at school came over to help us scour the place and paint. Victor Lasky, uncle of my maid of honor, and his wife lived in Somerville. They were our first contacts in Boston and took us under their wings. They were our tour guides, taking us to see the Old North Church and Paul Revere's house. We climbed the Bunker Hill Monument and ate oysters at the Union Oyster House. Victor came to help us paint dressed in a blue business suit. When Ed suggested that he might ruin his suit, he said it was old anyway. After Victor had finished painting, his suit and the top of his bald head were speckled with paint.

Our largest expense was a sleeper sofa, and for that we went to Sears. The lighting in the store was completely different from that in our apartment, so when we got the sofa home the colors screamed with our walls. The delivery men had carried the sofa up four flights of stairs and weren't happy when I told them they had to take it back. "Lady, you don't exchange sofas like you do a dress!" they said. It was that or repaint the walls. Fortunately Sears obliged.

During Ed's freshman year at Boston College, our friend Dan Shea, who met Ed on their first day of class that September, would come over once a month to drive us to the market, where we stocked up on groceries. When the shopping was finished, we would treat ourselves to onion soup and indian pudding at Durgin Park.

Our first baby was due the end of August 1948. One day in the late spring, we had finished putting the supplies in the car and went in for lunch. Water was rushing down the streets from a heavy rain. The rain had become a downpour when we came out of the restaurant, so we started to run to the car. My foot slipped on a piece of wet cardboard and I slid into the water-filled gutter, jamming my back on the high curbing. Ed and Dan froze, leaving me lying in the gutter on my back. "Will somebody *please* help me up?" I asked. They swung into action, picked me up, and drove right to the doctor's office. The two of them paced up and down until the doctor came out to assure them that I was all right. The color then came back into their faces.

As the delivery date approached, we borrowed a crib that fit perfectly in the foyer, and, with our limited funds, purchased basic baby equipment. Gifts were gladly received, and before Christa arrived, we had everything necessary. Neither of us had had any experience with babies, and since our families were not near, Dr. Spock became our guide.

That would have been fine except Christa developed eating difficulties. I tried to nurse her; when that didn't work out, the doctor put her on a formula – then another, and another. Nothing seemed to agree with her, and one feeding would sometimes lead into the next because she ate so slowly. When she regurgitated, large fluffy puffs were propelled across the room. Children's Hospital did various tests on her. Finally she became so dehydrated that we had to leave her in the hospital. She was diagnosed as having infant diarrhea. We went back to the hospital later that day during visiting hours. A nurse told us which room she was in. We walked up and down the long room lined with cribs on both sides and couldn't find her.

In some distress, we checked again at the desk and were told which crib she was in. When we went in again, there she was, sitting in the middle of the crib in diapers and stretching out her arms to us. Her head had been shaved on both sides leaving only a little thatch down the middle, and tubes were inserted into her scalp, the means of feeding her glucose and water. No wonder we didn't recognize her! We were not prepared for the sight and were devastated at how forlorn she looked.

Time went by slowly. Christa would be a little better and have her fluid increased, but when she was given other nourishment, the vomiting and diarrhea started again. This went on for a month. All the drugs tried had no effect until Aureomycin, which was fairly new, was given to her. It took hold, and she began to improve. We were relieved and delighted, and couldn't wait to bring her home. She was seven months old and had been in the hospital for five weeks.

Our apartment was small, and since the summer of 1948 had been brutally hot, we decided to spend the summer of 1949 with Ed's parents in Waterbury, Connecticut. Christa would have a lovely yard to play in, and it would be wonderful for us to be with relatives and friends. But it meant giving up our apartment in Boston.

When September came, we still hadn't been able to find another place to live due to the postwar demand for housing. Frank Frisoli, a classmate of Ed's, lived in Cambridge near Dan Shea. His parents had a small but neat and clean attic room furnished with a bed and desk that they offered to Ed until we could find an apartment. As Dan could pick up Ed and Frank and take them in to school, it was very convenient.

Mrs. Frisoli would invite Christa and me to dinner when we came up to visit from Waterbury. I have always enjoyed eating and still remember her meals. Course after course was served. They were all so good, it was difficult not to try everything. Mr. Frisoli made his own wine and kept my glass full. "Have another, Gracie!" he'd say. They all laughed when Ed, concerned, said that my face was getting red.

Apartment hunting became a major problem. All of Ed's spare time was spent following up newspaper leads, checking rental signs, and calling apartment managers. Everyone we knew was trying to help. We had thought that we would be in our own place at least by Thanksgiving, but we became worried that we might not even have a place by Christmas. Ed was also working part-time and trying to visit us on some weekends. We both wrote every day. It was discouraging and taking a toll not only on the three of us but, I'm sure, on our friends and families as well.

At Boston College, Tom Antico, Ed's Spanish professor, was also doing all that he could to help. We had become very close to him and his wife, Shirley, and their daughter Theresa was just six months older

than Christa. (Tom and Shirley later became godparents for our youngest child, Betsy.) The dean and the librarian were also trying to help
us apply for veterans' housing, but since we were from out of state, the
veterans' housing department would not take Ed's application at first.
However, early in November our application for veterans' housing was
accepted. They stretched a point because Ed was going to school in
Massachusetts, and we had become voters there. But there was a long
waiting list.

Dan Shea had a friend working at Mayor Curley's home. She suggested that it might help if I could tell the mayor our story and have
Christa with me when I did. It was worth a try.

Early one morning, Dan drove us to the mayor's red brick Georgian
house on the Jamaicaway. His friend let us in and had us wait in the hall
at the foot of the stairs. When Mayor Curley came down for his breakfast, there we were. I explained our problem. He patted Christa on the
head and told me to leave my name and address. I left relieved that the
visit was over with and hoped that it might have some value.

Well, something worked. About a week later, a telegram was sent to
Ed in Cambridge. "This Authority is happy to advise that you appear
eligible for occupancy of its veterans' housing development (Columbia
Village, formerly Camp McKay). Please be at the management office,
220 Mt. Vernon Street near Columbia Station, Dorchester, on Tuesday,
December 13, 1949, prepared to make the deposit of $5.00 if you desire
occupancy. Boston Housing Authority, John J. Coleman, Chairman."

On that Tuesday, I came to Boston, and Ed and I took a bus out to
the project. It was a gloomy, dreary day, with light rain falling. We found
the manager's office and showed him the telegram. The housing project
was made up of barracks-type buildings. In fact, they were barracks that
housed soldiers and then Italian prisoners-of-war during World War II.
Each building had four units. Nothing had been done to enhance the
yards. A cement path led from each front door to a mutual walkway
leading to the road. Clotheslines patterned the backs.

The manager took us over to apartment 24 at 47 Strandview Road
and opened the door. We entered into a decent-sized room. Off to the
back was a large kitchen with an icebox and a big black oil stove. The
floor slanted, so later we discovered that the water from the pan under
the icebox would run down the floor and out the back door if one forgot
to empty it. There was a small bedroom and a bathroom, including a

shower stall. We were thrilled! We had an apartment for less money than we had been spending and one with more room. We even had a yard, and the beach was at the end of the road. We almost couldn't believe it.

The manager was amazed. "Gee," he said, "usually they look at these places and say, 'What a dump.'" We signed on the dotted line.

My uncle, Sylvan des Rochers, offered to move us back to Boston; he had moved us to Waterbury, sofa and all, the year before. My brother, Steve George, gave Christa an eight-week-old puppy, Teddy, of mixed origin. The pup settled in the large patch pocket of my camel hair coat for his trip to Boston. We were all excited and couldn't wait to get settled. It was December 16, 1949. We were going to have Christmas in our own place!

We scoured, scrubbed, and painted. Christa had a wonderful time "helping" and playing with her puppy. On one wall, we put vivid red Chinese design wallpaper. Our black painted table and chairs against the wall made a smart dining area. The bedroom was Christa's. She had a small bed and a dresser, a bright blue upholstered rocking chair, a table for her record player, and a toy box.

The oil stove was a challenge and had to be kept going during the cold weather because it provided our heat and hot water. The shower stall was an ugly tin affair that we painted black and stenciled with gilt letter C's down the side. We thought it looked sharp.

Ed's mother and father drove up Christmas Eve; the table was set with wedding presents – linen, china, silver, and candles. The menu was shrimp cocktail and lobster. After Christa was put to bed, we brought in the tree, the biggest, fullest one we could find to fit into the room, and spent the remainder of the evening decorating it. Teddy found his special place to sleep – under the tree between presents.

After the big splurge, it was back to reality. The neighbors that we met were nice, mostly blue-collar working people, a handful of students, and quite a few children. The neighbor whose apartment butted against Christa's bedroom stopped us one day to ask, "Do you know that your little girl sometimes gets up during the night? She puts on the record player, and we can hear her rocking and singing nursery rhymes." We had to admit that we did not hear her and apologized for the disturbance. "Not at all," he replied. "It's no problem. I get home from work during the night. Just thought you might like to know."

Weekends we would play bridge with Bob O'Connor and Betty Hedlund. They were getting married that year, and Bob had a new movie camera that he wanted to try out before the honeymoon. That spring we put up a swing set for Christa in the backyard, and Bob practiced by shooting an entire roll of film showing Christa swinging – back and forth, back and forth, back and forth, and every once in a while I would step into view to give her a push. We had a lot of laughs over that at Bob's expense, accusing him of trying to make us seasick.

We spent the hot days of summer on the beach. Teddy and Christa were inseparable. Friends came visiting. Our apartment became a great place for Ed's classmates – they gathered there to study for exams. And Christa learned to sing "For Boston."

Grandma and Christa

Ed's mother was elated when Christa was born. She finally had a little girl she could pamper and dress in pretty clothes. And Christa seemed to understand pampering. When she was about two years old, Christa found she could hold her breath when she didn't get her way. It worried us that she would hurt herself, and it was scary to see her turn blue, but her pediatrician assured us that she could not harm herself. One day, when visiting her grandmother, Christa had a tantrum and held her breath. We were in Mom's kitchen, so I sat her on a chair and told her to stay there until she behaved herself. Christa passed out and fell off the chair. She wasn't hurt and had caught her breath, but it sure made me feel like a terrible mother. And I know I didn't earn any Brownie points with my mother-in-law!

Mom loved to take Christa out shopping or visiting to show her off. They became great friends. Christa spoke very easily and could carry on a conversation. When she was a toddler, her grandmother would take her to the country club for lunch. Mom's nephew was the manager there, and everyone would make a great fuss over Christa. They would keep her talking and would delight in listening to her Boston accent. Mom was so proud of her, and Christa looked forward to the times she spent with her grandmother.

Christa was a precocious child, and although she was happy with her brothers and friends, we felt she needed something of her own to do. So, when she was four years old, I enrolled her in modeling classes. They were fun and good training in posture and manners. One day, I was asked if she would be allowed to be in a fashion show on a New Haven television station.

We had just bought our first television set, so Ed decided to stay home with our sons to watch the show. A neighbor came over with her two daughters to see Christa on television, too.

Christa and I drove to New Haven, arriving, as asked, a half hour early. Christa was taken off to a dressing room, and I was shown to a room where I would be able to see the show on a monitor. As Christa made her entrance, the commentator introduced her, "And this little blond is Christa Corrigan – what a lovely name!"

On the way home, Christa chattered about how bright the lights were and how nice everyone was. She dashed into the house, "Daddy, did you see me? Did you like the clothes I was wearing?"

Almost as soon as we walked in, the phone rang with a call from my brother's wife, Helen. "What happened to Christa's hair?" she asked. "I told my friends to watch for my niece on the show and said they would recognize her by her blond, bouncy curls." Christa's hair had just been cut in a short pixie – no curls!

We bought our first home and moved outside Boston to Framingham in 1954. Ed's parents drove up frequently to visit. Christa's dog, Teddy, was able to tell when their car was coming before they were even in sight. He'd scamper from the house and cut across the field to meet them. They would pull over, and Teddy would jump into the car. Then a short time later they would all arrive with Teddy hanging his head out the car window and panting.

Christa's other Aunt Helen – Ed's brother Jim's wife – recalls the time when Christa was a few years older and visiting in Waterbury. They were playing cards, and Mom kept making mistakes. "Christa looked up at me, her eye contact telling me not to let on. She wanted her grandmother to feel good."

When Lisa was born on June 23, 1957, Ed brought me a letter from Christa while I was still in the hospital:

Dear Mommy, I hope you are feeling better. I can't wait to see the baby. I was so glad when Daddy said it was a girl. Mommy, when we were going to Grama's house, Teddy chased the car. So we let him come, too. Hope you come home soon. Love, Christa.

She had written it on a plain piece of paper, drawing the lines with a ruler and pen. She was eight years old.

Years later, after Christa married and moved to Maryland, she would often stop in Waterbury on her way home from Framingham. One October, after spending her birthday with us, she wrote:

You wouldn't believe my grand exit yesterday from Connecticut. First I packed the car, said good-bye to everyone and locked the keys in the car! So, Aunt Helen got a fork and knife, and we pried open the vent window that was already bent from two break-ins. Then I said good-bye again, got in the car, and it wouldn't start. Two hours and one new battery (compliments of Grandma) later, I was finally on my way. The old battery had two dead cells in it, and if it stalled, the car had to be jumped to restart; I was hoping that I could run it to Maryland and then Steve could get a battery at Sears and install it, but the man at the station said it would really be too risky. (He sounded sincere, so I figured I better believe him.) What really irritated me was the price – $36.00! I wanted the least expensive one since I had some money with me, but they only had the vw size in the expensive model. He did call two other gas stations for me.

Naturally, Grandma wouldn't take a check or any of my money – she even gave me an extra $20 in case I had trouble on the way home. I really felt guilty about it, especially since I also got a beautiful sweater and slacks set – also a necklace! And Aunt Helen bought me the parka and gave me draperies and a spread and pillows. [Some were birthday presents.]

Mom's eyesight began failing, and she was living alone after Ed's father died. His brother Jim lived over an hour away, and we were worried about her. We had been trying to get her to live with us for over a year, but she wouldn't give up her home and her independence. She would visit, but then she wanted to go home to take care of things. Once Christa went to visit her and found that her grandmother was unable to watch television because of poor reception. So Christa went to the hardware store, bought some antenna wire, attached it to the antenna, threaded it through the attic window, brought it back into the house through the living room window, and attached it to the television set. It worked.

We finally persuaded Mom to move in with us. Together we sold her house, keeping just the pieces of furniture she wanted. Christa, who by then lived in New Hampshire, was to have her grandmother's mahogany dining room table and eight chairs. She was thrilled to have it since it fit so beautifully in her Victorian house. She already had her grandmother's twelve-piece place settings of china.

Mom was relieved to be rid of the worries of running a house and having stairs to climb. We loved having her with us and not worrying about her being alone. We fixed up her room – new carpeting and wallpaper with draperies to match. She had her comfortable chair, television, desk, and telephone. Her room was a cozy place to get away from the hubbub of the family if she chose.

Christa's Scott and Caroline were Mom's first great-grandchildren. They would visit her in her room, climb on the bed, or share the rocking chair. They entertained each other with their stories. Jessie, our dog, also found a haven in Grandma's room. There were always treats on the dresser or in the desk drawer.

Before Caroline's first Christmas, Christa made an appointment with a photographer. She wanted the four generations of Corrigan women captured in a photograph for posterity: Stella Adams Corrigan, Grace George Corrigan, Christa Corrigan McAuliffe, and Caroline Corrigan McAuliffe. Christa had the pictures framed for all of us.

Family, Names, and Identity

Christa was Irish, Lebanese, German, English, and American Indian. Her Corrigan name came from her Irish grandfather. Her paternal grandmother was English and American Indian. My father's family was Lebanese and my mother's was German. My mother died shortly after the birth of my brother, Steve, when I was three. Steve and I were brought up by our maternal grandparents together with their five surviving children in Waterbury, Connecticut. My father, an engineer working for Consolidated Edison on the Hill Gate Power Station in New York City, would visit as often as he could, and we would spend part of our summer vacations with him.

I was ten years old and my brother was eight when our father was killed in an automobile accident that occurred while he was driving up from New York to spend Thanksgiving with us. When the family went to close up his apartment, they found that it had been completely ransacked. Nothing was left. He had been a handball and tennis champion, besides excelling at golf and baseball, but his trophies and all mementos were gone.

In 1984, my Aunt Mary sent me a picture of my father that I had never seen before; I was absolutely delighted. It was his picture taken for the yearbook when he graduated from New York University. I was glad to be able to give a copy to each of our children and to my brother and his children. Christa was particularly pleased. From the photo, she was convinced that her son Scott's large, dark eyes came from his great-grandfather.

Christa never knew my parents, of course, but as the first great-grand-child, she did have a wonderful relationship with my grandmother Harder when she was little. And we maintained ties with my brother, Steve, his wife, Helen, and their three daughters, Marcia, Marion, and Linda, who are around our children's ages. They lived in Connecticut, so we didn't live near enough to be together often, but we always felt close.

The last time we were all together was for Marion's wedding. Christa came up from Houston to attend. Marcia told Christa that her son Matthew's teacher hadn't believed him when he said his cousin was the Teacher in Space. His first-grade teacher thought he was just telling a tale when he also said that Christa was coming to visit. Christa immediately pulled out one of her NASA pictures and wrote on it, "To my cousin Matthew, Reach for the Stars! Love, Christa." The teacher was so excited when she saw the photo she called the local paper – later a grinning Matt appeared on the front page holding up Christa's photo.

Both Christa and I had name problems. Until I married, I went by Grace Mary George. I discovered then that my birth certificate was made out to Jewel Mae George, after my paternal grandmother, Julia, and maternal grandmother, Mary. My mother was ill and unable to leave the hospital until I was six months old. She considered it the grace of God that she lived, so I was baptized Grace Harder (her maiden name) George. After my marriage, I began to use the name Grace George Corrigan.

When I was pregnant with Christa, we decided that if we had a boy, we would name him Christopher, which was Ed's middle name. When our first baby was a girl, we chose Christa, a derivation of Christopher, for her middle name and Sharon for her first. At that time, the Catholic Church required a saint's name for baptism. Ed felt we had that covered. We'd just tell the priest that her middle name was Christ with an *a* added. He would never question that!

For six months, we called our baby Sheri Christa. We even had our

Christmas cards printed that way. She was very blond, and we became fond of the name Christa, thinking somehow that it really suited her better. So we just dropped the Sharon. It took a little while, but soon everyone was using the name Christa. We never thought of her as anything but Christa after that. We simply forgot to tell any of this to Christa.

We didn't want *Christa* shortened to *Chris*. At times we would emphasize the last syllable of her name – perhaps too often. Once during a shopping trip Christa became separated from us. We had stressed to the children the importance of finding a person in charge, such as a policeman or salesclerk, if they should ever become lost, and Christa followed this advice. We were frantically looking around the department store when the loudspeaker announced, "We have a little five year old with blond hair and brown eyes who is looking for her family. Her name is Chris Ta."

Before Christa's confirmation, she had to take her baptismal certificate to the church. She became quite upset when she discovered her baptismal name was Sharon Christa. "But I haven't been using my legal name – won't it make a difference in my records?" She solved this by signing her name S. Christa Corrigan. Many a time she would receive mail addressed to Sister Christa.

When she filled out the application for the Teacher-in-Space program, she was strongly tempted to leave off the *Sharon* but decided her application might be rejected for being incomplete. Later she found out that Nicki Wenger, one of the ten finalists, used her nickname on the application.

Some friends, even relatives, and many acquaintances were taken by surprise as then Vice President George Bush announced that Sharon McAuliffe was the Teacher in Space. For some, it was only much later that they connected Sharon with the Christa that they knew.

When Christa was married, it was not as popular as it is now for a woman to keep her maiden name. After attending a wedding at which the bride kept her maiden name, Christa said she wished she had. Not being of her generation, I didn't like the idea. It seemed to me that it would definitely complicate matters, especially with children.

After Christa and Steve had moved to Maryland, Christa wrote, "We opened a joint checking account; since we just got married, there is no service charge for a year! I still haven't gotten used to my name – I signed the papers at the bank in my maiden name! And when anyone asks me, I always say 'Corrigan.' I guess it takes time."

When I wrote back, I told Christa about the time I was similarly embarrassed: I was just about due with our third child, Stephen. My obstetrician was a Boston College alumnus who invited us to a large BC dinner party. There I introduced myself as Grace George. Ed quickly supplied the "Corrigan."

Christa felt that family and background were very important and that people could gain a wealth of information by tracing their roots. She spent a great deal of time questioning her paternal grandmother about her family. When her maternal great-aunt was living with Christa and Steve in Maryland, she had many a conversation about the German side of the family. Christa wanted to leave a family history for her children. She and Steve decided that both Scott and Caroline should have Corrigan as their middle name to establish an important family link.

Kit's Birth

Ed and I had arranged to meet at Dr. Barton's office on Beacon street one spring day in 1951. Christa and I were to come in by trolley from Dorchester, and Ed was to come from his classes at Boston College. I was more than seven months pregnant and due for a checkup. Since Ed was to graduate before the baby's birth and would soon be working, we felt we could afford a private doctor and a private room at the Richardson House. When Christa was born, Ed was just starting his sophomore year, so I went through the clinic of the Boston Lying In Hospital. There wasn't room for any extras in our budget then.

Since Christa and I were a little early, I decided to shop for something special for dinner. When we arrived at the doctor's office, I was carrying a brown grocery bag with a loaf of French bread sticking out. Christa was wearing her storm coat with a fur collar, and her curls were tucked up under a bright red tam. When Ed arrived, he gave her a big hug and took my bag.

We sat on a striped satin sofa while I waited for my turn. Suddenly, I just didn't feel right and decided to tell the nurse at the reception desk. When I stood up I was embarrassed to see a wet spot on the lovely sofa. Without any hesitation, she whipped me through the doors of the office, and before I knew it, I was on the table and the doctor was examining me. He told me that I would have to go to the hospital right away because I might be giving birth shortly. If I did not give birth in a few days, I could go home, but I would have to stay in bed because there was danger of infection following the rupture of my membranes. He explained as gently as he could that this child was too little to survive. I tried to explain to him that I carry this way.

When the doctor told Ed, Ed didn't believe we would lose the baby. "Grace wasn't much bigger when Christa was born, and Christa weighed seven pounds, thirteen and a half ounces!"

I protested. How could I go to the hospital now? How could I stay off my feet for two months with a little girl to care for? I just wasn't prepared! Of course, prepared or not, we were sent off in a taxi to the hospital – we three and the bag of groceries.

Children were not allowed above the first floor of the hospital, so Ed had to stay with Christa. I kissed Christa goodbye, and since everything happened so fast, I asked Ed to come up to see me when I got settled. There seemed to be so much yet to plan. I was scooted right into bed. It was a long time before Ed appeared. "What a time I had getting away!" he said. "I explained to Christa that I just wanted to see you for a few minutes before we went home. I asked her to sit right there and not to move until I got back. She'd say, 'Okay, Daddy,' I'd walk to the elevator, and then she'd call after me, 'I'm not going to sit here!' This went on a few more times, and I was ready to give up when an obviously pregnant, well-dressed woman came into the foyer and sized up the situation. She offered to sit with Christa because she wasn't really in a hurry – she was to have a caesarean section the next day. So here I am, but I can't stay!"

The next day, Ed stayed home from school, and a neighbor came in to stay with Christa while he visited me. He reported, "Everything is going along all right. I asked Christa what she would like for breakfast, and she said an egg. So I cooked eggs for us. I had no idea how to tell if they were done, and so I kept them in the pan until the edges got sort of black. But she rose to the occasion, saying, 'Daddy, you're a good cooker.'"

By the end of the second day, I was still being monitored constantly, and nothing was happening. Ed had brought a *Redbook* magazine for me; and that evening, I read the novel at the back of the magazine. Entitled *The Return of Christopher,* it was a poignant story about a young boy who was named Christopher, after his uncle. Christopher admired his uncle and wanted to be just like him when he grew up. Since the family had always called his uncle "Kit," young Christopher was pleased and proud when his family started calling him Kit. Ed and I had planned on the name Christopher if this baby was a boy, and now we had a nickname for him, one that wouldn't confuse Christa with Christopher.

About five o'clock the next morning, I awoke, feeling again as if something different was happening. When I rang for the nurse, I suddenly had all kinds of attention and was wheeled out of the room, down the corridor, and into the delivery room. By ten o'clock that morning, I had delivered a four-and-a-half-pound baby boy.

When I was finally awake and saw the doctor, all I could say was, "Thank you, thank you." He just grinned and said, "Don't thank *me, you* did it. It's difficult to believe the baby is so big!"

Kit was in an incubator on the floor below me. They wouldn't allow me to go to see him, so I had to rely on Ed and our pediatrician, Dr. Olga Allens, to assure me that he was a fine, healthy boy.

It wasn't until five days later when I was discharged from the hospital that I could go to the nursery and see the baby for the first time. He was a long, skinny little thing lying in his incubator. It was a strange feeling to be allowed to see him through the nursery window only, and not be permitted to hold him and take him home. We had to wait until he reached five pounds – probably within a month.

Our friend Dan Shea was waiting for us in his car. Christa was with him bouncing up and down with excitement. She asked all kinds of questions about her baby brother. We had to describe exactly how he looked and explain why he had to stay in the hospital. She accepted that she would have to wait to see him and was really glad that at least I could come home. Kit eventually came home the week before Ed graduated from Boston College; Christa was two and a half years old.

Childhood

Christa loved the new babies as they arrived, and helped with their care. Any time Christa would be away overnight, visiting friends, at camp, or at her grandmother's, she always brought back small presents for her brothers and sisters; and as she got older and went on dates, the girls would find little things tucked near their pillows the next morning. A piece of gum, candy, Golden Books, sometimes a flower.

Her letters from Girl Scout camp always reflected fun and enjoyment, and she described both her accomplishments and relationships with the other girls and counselors. Excerpts from her 1959 letters include:

"I got your letters and a card from Grandma with a dollar in it. One dollar is enough so you don't have to send anymore money.

I am having lots of fun. Today we are going on a Hobo hike. We are going to take sandwiches, pop and fruit. We are going to hike a long time. Bertie was having trouble. First she sat on the bench and it sunk. So Stretch put a flat stone under the bench and when Bertie sat on it the stone broke in three pieces! Then I found a board and we put that over the stone and Bertie decided to eat standing up!

I hung my uniform up and almost all the wrinkles are out of it!

Tonight we are going to have a sleepout and a cookout. For dessert we are going to have chocolate dips – you take a stick and stick a marshmallow on it and leave it on wax paper in the shade. Then, you make fudge and while it is still hot, dip your marshmallow in it and wait till it cools. Sounds good, doesn't it?

Thursday night we are going to have a foil dinner of potatoes, carrots, and a hamburger pattie. Yummy!!! The mail has been coming fine. I have already gotten six letters, one postcard and one card. I hope the mail has been coming in all right at home.

We went out into the boats today and I rowed some. Twice we were almost beached. I have already taken seven pictures. Today I took one of all the girls in our unit and all the counselors.

One thing I'm not enjoying is that there is a girl named Rachel, she's nice but always makes fun of Charlene because she's bigger than all of us and has to undress under a bathrobe and she wears a bra, so Rachel hid her bathrobe under my bed and Charlene's raincoat under Kathy's and is always making fun of her or saying, "Charlie dear." But everyone else is alright.

Last night I had to go to sleep and missed a fashion show because I couldn't swallow and had a headache.

I learned to dive and love to do it.

I'd find little things around Christa's room, like apple cores, candy wrappers rolled up together with stockings that hadn't made it to the hamper, or sometimes an ice cream dish and spoon in a desk drawer so I wouldn't know she had been eating ice cream. During her high school years, she struggled with a weight problem. Later on she would still have that problem but kept it under control by jogging and all her other activities. She loved to eat as I do, and the bane of her life was that I never gained any weight. Christa and Betsy both had to watch their weight, while Lisa and I didn't have that problem.

Her brother Steve used to refer to Christa as "Big Christa," as in "we always have to do what Big Christa says." Christa was three and a half years older than Steve, and we would at times leave her in charge of the boys when she was old enough to baby-sit.

Christa was teacher and mentor to her younger sisters. Lisa and Betsy remember always being an integral part of her life. She gave love, time, and caring to their relationship. As an adventure, Christa would sometimes give them change and take them on a bus downtown so they could shop.

Christa taught Betsy and Lisa to sew. Ed and I gave Christa a sewing machine for her sixteenth birthday, and that Christmas she made me a red velvet hostess gown with scooped neckline, empire waist, and sleeves edged with white lace. It fit beautifully. From then on, she made many things, frequently surprising the girls and me with a new outfit. From lining jackets to making buttonholes, Christa enjoyed sewing, and whatever she made was lovely and always a perfect fit.

Christa taught her sisters to knit and play the guitar, but most important, she taught them to be kind and generous to others. Once Lisa went with Christa to a friend's home, and noticed a picture of a young man with long hair on the mantelpiece. Lisa made a disapproving face, and Christa said, "Lisa, I'm surprised at you – judging people on their appearance." Lisa thought, "Geez, Christa, I'm only nine!"

Christa's brothers and sisters as children and as adults had immense respect for Christa; a difficult problem might be faced with the thought "Now what would Christa do in this situation?"

Love for Music, Love for Life

When Christa was a baby, we sang to her all the time. Her father had a good voice. He was a boy soprano and had sung solo on stage and radio. I usually can't sing on key, and most of the time I don't know it! Christa's favorite songs were "I Love You a Bushel and a Peck" and "A – You're Adorable." Ed played the piano and as Christa became older, she would come in to sing or just to listen. He played well, and when anyone would comment on his training, Ed would answer, "Four years of lessons as a child." Then I'd get chided because I had taken the same amount of lessons and could just render "Chopsticks."

I also took a lot of kidding about my singing – and not just from my own family! After teaching my Brownie troop a Girl Scout song, the little girl from next door went home and sang the song. Her mother asked, "That's nice, Barbara, but is that the way the song goes, or is that the way Mrs. Corrigan sings it?"

Christa took piano lessons from Mr. Bordeaux, who was quite a taskmaster. He put up with no nonsense and demanded complete discipline. At age eleven, Christa played for the National Federation Festival, receiving a score of 94 with examiners' comments that "she has a very good tone, and her interpretation of the nocturne is excellent."

Mr. Bordeaux was pleased with her progress but demanded much more time than Christa felt she was able to give. It was with reluctance that she gave up her lessons. She continued to play the piano, but started to concentrate on the guitar.

Christa then took over teaching songs to the Girl Scout troop, accompanying herself on the guitar. She became involved in every musical she was able to, whether it was put on by school, church, or community. Sometimes she sang solo, sometimes in the chorus.

For the Marian High School senior class play, Christa played the part of Sister Margaretta in the *Sound of Music*. Lisa and Betsy went to the school to try out for the parts of the younger children. They both have good, clear voices, but they were too shy and couldn't sing out strongly enough for the stage. Ed's mother and my Aunt Frances came up from Connecticut to see the musical. During intermission, Christa, in her nun's habit, played the vibraphone with the orchestra. We didn't even know Christa could play the vibraphone!

Christa sang all through college with the choir and had parts in many of their musicals. As a sophomore, she played Kate, one of General Stanley's daughters in *The Pirates of Penzance*.

After being in Maryland a year, she wrote, "I might join a Madrigal Choir at one of the local junior colleges. It meets every Thursday night.

I really miss the training I had in college every week. My voice has taken a downward plunge. I can just about reach D! Sue Rowald [her friend] was thinking of joining also. It should be fun." It was.

In another of her letters she wrote, "One of the teachers who used to work here had her Master's Degree piano recital at Howard University yesterday. It was so good. The pieces were challenging and Helen was superb. The only bad part was the piano. It was not in tune and the tone was not great. It's a shame they didn't have a Yamaha!" For our twenty-fifth wedding anniversary, my gift to Ed was a Yamaha baby grand. Christa loved it.

She belonged to the Junior Service League after moving to Concord, New Hampshire, and we went to all their musicals. The last one we saw was *Little Red Riding Hood and the Monkey Flower Wolf.* Christa played the part of Granny Greenthumb and looked impressive hobbling around the stage. With her hair sprayed gray and makeup including age lines on her face, we joked that now we knew what she would look like when she got old. She reminded me so much of my Aunt Frances.

The morning that the selection committee was to make their Teacher-in-Space choice, Ed came into the kitchen where I was making breakfast and said with a strange expression on his face, "You know what I just remembered? Christa singing one of her favorite songs while I played for her. How's this for a good omen?" Ed went over to the piano to find the sheet music for André Previn's "You're Gonna Hear from Me." "Just listen to the words," he said:

> Move over sun and give me some sky,
> I've got some wings that I'm eager to try,
> I may be unknown – but wait till I've flown,
> You're gonna hear from me!

New York City

In 1964, we took our children – Christa, Kit, Stephen, Lisa, and Betsy – to the New York World's Fair. My great-aunt Carrie invited us to stay with her at her apartment on First Avenue in New York City.

Aunt Carrie was a first-generation American of German descent. She was a great opera buff, had a magnificent singing voice, and, when younger, had been in demand, especially to sing in churches. She was sixty-three years old when she sang beautifully at our wedding.

She still went to the office every day, traveled extensively, and was a stubborn Democrat. Aunt Carrie never married, but she always knew what was best for her brother's children (my aunts and uncles) and then for my brother and me. By the time our children were born, Aunt Carrie had mellowed a bit.

She was very good to all her nieces and nephews. When one reached the proper age, he or she would be treated to a trip to New York and given a tour of the city, a boat ride around the island, a trip to the Statue of Liberty, a visit to the Empire State Building, and a walk around Rockefeller Center. Saturday afternoon was spent at a matinee at the Metropolitan Opera followed by a German dinner at Luchow's.

Christa, Kit, and Stephen had all been given the tour of Manhattan. But this was the first experience of the city for five-year-old Betsy and six-year-old Lisa. We had ten days to see the sights, including the World's Fair. Everyone was excited about the vacation.

After settling in at the apartment, we walked over to a large old church in the neighborhood. Only a few people were about. As we walked toward the altar, we thought we could hear a baby whimpering, but no one was holding a baby. A few rows from the altar, we discovered a baby all wrapped in blankets lying in a pew.

The children wanted me to pick up the baby, and insisted, "The baby is crying! It wants to be picked up." Ed and I tried to explain that the baby was not crying – except for an occasional whimper, it seemed quite content – and that people just couldn't pick up a baby that didn't belong to them. "We will wait. The mother must be here someplace."

Still no one was coming around, and the children kept insisting that we do something. They said no one wanted the baby, and they wanted to take it home and keep it. They began making plans: "We'll take the baby home." "The baby can sleep in Christa's room." "We'll take turns caring for it." And on and on.

When we said that you just can't take a baby that doesn't belong to you, they wanted us to do whatever it is you have to do to keep it. They were convinced that no one else wanted it.

Ed and I said to each other, "This is crazy – they are all set to take this baby, go home, and give up their vacation. And they think we're terrible for not jumping at the chance to increase our family!"

Just then, two policemen came in the front of the church and rushed down the aisle to where we were watching the baby. A priest came running in from the back. From their conversation, we learned that the mother had called the police station to alert them that she had left the baby and tell them exactly where it was. She felt she could no longer care for the baby. The priest seemed to know who the mother was, so they took the baby, assuring everyone that they would all work to help the mother keep her child. At this point a small crowd had gathered.

The baby taken care of, we left the church. The children were disappointed not to have another brother or sister (we never found out which), but were all excited and happy that the baby would be with its mother. Ed and I were still more than a little amazed at the children's reaction to the situation.

The World's Fair was wonderful: we were greeted by the sight of the huge unisphere at the main mall, the lunar fountain, and the solar fountain. It was called the Fair of the Century, and it gave us fascinating glimpses of the future. We tasted for the first time Belgian waffles heaped with strawberries and whipped cream. We went on the flume ride, the Swiss sky ride, and the boat ride. We went in and out of exhibits, Christa with Betsy and Lisa at her side, the boys running ahead, and Ed and I following behind.

We stood on the moving walkway and looked in awe at Michelangelo's *Pietà*. We admired a teal blue Bonneville convertible displayed with dramatic lighting on a revolving stage. Would a family with five children want or have a car that elegant? (That fall, we bought the very same model, same color, and have never had another car that we all enjoyed more!)

We went to Radio City Music Hall and saw the Rockettes and Debbie Reynolds in *The Unsinkable Molly Brown*. Afterward, we were on to Mama Leone's for one of her wonderful Italian dinners.

We were getting saturated with everything to see and do, but we wanted to make one more stop before returning home. This was to the home of my father's oldest sister, Mary, and her husband, Dr. Philip Hitti. They lived in Princeton, New Jersey, where my uncle taught at the university.

That afternoon, Aunt Mary introduced us to tabouleh, a salad made from bulgur wheat and finely chopped vegetables. "In Lebanon," she explained, "young people serve and eat this at their parties, the same as young people in this country serve pizza at theirs." We all enjoyed the tabouleh so much that I have made it ever since. The problem then was that it was not popular as it is now, and I had difficulty buying the wheat. When Aunt Mary went to New York for her supply, she would send me some. Later, when Christa and Steve were living in Maryland, Christa wrote, "We were in Georgetown Saturday and went into the coffee, tea, and spice house for some bagels. I saw a sack of wheat pilaf and it looked like the grain needed for tabouleh. Then I spotted the recipe! I bought a pound of the wheat – I can't wait to make the salad!"

Christa and Steve made tabouleh often, not only for themselves, but also for friends, and would take some along to parties. Christa wrote about the great comments and compliments she would receive, especially from those who knew of tabouleh and were pleasantly surprised that she knew how to make it.

Besides learning how to make tabouleh, we brought home some charcoal studies of the children that were sketched at the fair. They hung in our hallway until each child had his or her own home. Now Christa's children see her portrait hanging in the hallway of their home in Concord, New Hampshire.

Girl Scout Camp

In July 1965, Christa left for the Girl Scout Round-Up in Farragut, Idaho – a gathering of 12,000 Girl Scouts from forty countries camping together. While on the trip, Christa wrote the following letters home:

July 12, 1965. Right now we're in Illinois and Central time – as usual I've forgotten something – my sunglasses. We stopped in Chicago today and visited the Art Museum. You wouldn't believe Chicago. It's wild. The buildings are so modern it's unbelievable. The train is a riot. It seems as if we just got over one meal and we have to stand in line for the next; the meals are pretty good though.

In Chicago we changed trains (just engines and dining cars) so we ate in an open car. If you don't think that's hard on the digestion, you should try it.

All you can see across Ohio, Indiana, and Illinois is flat land, corn and farms. I really appreciate New England . . . I didn't sleep at all last night, we weren't talking or anything but the train was so bumpy.

Right now we're in Minnesota and so far the scenery is still the same. The air conditioning is out in our car, it feels like the underworld . . . We stopped in St. Paul last night and another train hitched onto ours.

July 15. We arrived today! It's so big and there are so many girls. We had a huge welcome at the train station with a band and all the townspeople waving banners and wishing us a good time.

We arrived at the site around noon and as of now (10:10) we still aren't completely set up.

Yellowstone Park was beautiful with all the geysers and springs. Tell Kit I got him some rocks to add to his collection and Lisa and Betsy something from Smokey the Bear [Christa had bought her sisters dolls, and with her Girl Scout friends made garters for them on the train home] . . . I took my first cold shower after four days. Layers of dirt came off . . . Alzira [a girl scout from Brazil who had stayed with us the month before the Round-Up] sends her love and says to keep the letters coming – thanks for writing – say hi to everyone – I miss you all.

July 16. Round Up is really great   the girls arrived from Kansas and Illinois today. We helped them set up camp. I feel like a celebrity. Just today I must have had my picture taken ten times for various newspapers. I also sent in my press release, just made the deadline!

We put on our demonstrations of block printing today . . . You wouldn't believe the tumbleweed, it's all over the place. We have two trading posts – they have everything!

July 19. We've been pretty busy. We were filmed for a TV show. It was so beautiful and patriotic, the girls in uniform marching with flags of their countries. Daniel Secunda, the producer for United Artists explained all about recording. He hopes to get a couple of 45s recorded and the Girl Scouts on the Hit Parade! For Stephen and Kit's benefit, he directed the two Beatles movies.

Today we went on a conservation tour through the National Forest. We were given pamphlets and two pine cones with the seeds so Mom, if you want pine trees – I have the beginnings. The winds and dust are terrific. The scenery is so beautiful I wish I could put it in a box and take it home to share with all of you. With so many trails to climb and forums to attend it's tiring just to fit everything into your schedule. I hope to get to the career forum on the Peace Corps today. The group right next to us has six guitars and one banjo – they play extremely well. We are teaching each other new songs. Practice makes perfect and sore fingers.

July 21. Only five full days of camping left! Time passes so fast here with so much to do. Alzira has met a couple of counselors from Brazil. They are coming to supper tonight.

I have been picked with some other girls to be in a flag ceremony. It is impressive, an avenue of flags. I will be carrying the flag of Dahomey (an African country). Tell the kids that I saw some prairie dogs and gophers yesterday and today. They are so fast and tiny, it's fun to watch them.

July 24. My train is coming in at 9:30 a.m. Friday. It's really terrible to be thinking of leaving because no one wants to go. The girls from Illinois will give us a goodbye breakfast as a return for our welcome dinner. I'm in the Catholic choir and will be singing at Mass tomorrow morning. Last week Mass was at 6:30 and the Protestant service was at 8:30. This week we are switched around. See you Friday!

High School and a Motorbike

Christa had a full, happy, and fairly normal high school career; she did well in class and got along with her teachers and classmates, enjoying her extracurricular activities as well. As a junior she played on the Marian High School junior varsity girls' basketball team, and also was the pitcher for St. Jeremiah's softball team. In 1964 they won the Deanery Championships. Barbara Cmar Eldridge was the catcher for the parish team.

Barbara and Christa were sitting together in the bus going to school February 21, 1962. The day before Marian High had canceled school so everyone could watch while Lt. Col. John Glenn made his historic flight on *Friendship 7*, orbiting the earth three times before landing safely in the Atlantic Ocean.

They discussed the wonder of the flight, and Christa said to Barbara, "Do you realize that someday people will be going to the moon? Maybe even taking a *bus,* and *I* want to do that!"

Although no rebel, Christa didn't hesitate to ignore convention when she believed it was warranted; she caused a minor sensation by wearing the first strapless gown ever seen at a Marian High School dance.

When she was old enough, Christa took after-school jobs to help with Marian High School's tuition charges; she and Steve McAuliffe both worked for a time at a cleaners about a mile down the street. It would be dark in the winter when Christa came home from work, so Ed or I would meet her at the bus stop; we assumed she was walking to work from school. When Ed found out that Steve was giving her a ride to work on the back of his motorbike, Ed forbade her to travel that way. We thought that she was abiding by his wishes until the telephone rang one afternoon.

"This is the Framingham Union Hospital calling. Can you come to take your daughter home?"

"Is she all right? What happened? Why is she there?"

"She will be fine, she's scraped up a bit, especially the leg that she landed on when the motorbike fell over in the accident."

Well –

Later, Steve McAuliffe also had a motorbike for transportation while he was going to Georgetown Law School. When it was no longer needed he offered it to our son Steve. Naturally, our Steve was delighted even though his father wasn't.

To get the motorbike to Framingham from her home in Maryland, Christa had a hitch put on the Volkswagen and connected the motorbike to the hitch. When she reached the first toll booth on the New Jersey Turnpike she was told that she wasn't allowed to trail anything on her car while on the turnpike. She convinced the toll booth operator that she was only going to the next exit, she would definitely get off then, and could she please just go that far? She played this game at every toll gate. When she finally reached home, she handed the bike over to her brother, saying, "I hope you appreciate what I went through getting this to you!"

College Years

One evening when all our children happened to be at home, I looked around at them sitting at the dinner table and remarked how nice it was that they all had gone on to college and graduated.

Christa gave me that sideways glance of hers and said, "As if we had a choice!" "Christa, you know I never pressured any of you . . ." I looked at my husband for help. Ed just shrugged as Christa answered, "Come on, Ma, you know you were conditioning us right from the start." They were all shaking their heads in agreement. It was a revelation to me.

Because their last names began with the letter C, Bette Chase, Joanne Connor, and Christa Corrigan became fast friends at Framingham State College. This friendship started when they found themselves seated beside each other in all the same classes. They were also commuters and didn't share the same day-to-day closeness that the dorm students developed among themselves. As a result, the three girls formed their own "away from school" relationship.

Joanne, driving her old black Volkswagen, would pick up Christa and then Bette on her way to school. They made use of that time to hash over their studies.

Christa conned Joanne into joining the chorus with her. When they had practice, Bette would wait for them to finish for her ride home. One day she decided to wait in the hall. The choral director saw her and beckoned her to join them. "If you are here, you are going to sing!" So then the three of them belonged to the chorus.

They used their strengths to help each other. Bette excelled in math and made that subject easier for Christa to understand. When Joanne had mononucleosis, Bette and Christa took turns climbing up to the third floor to read the meters at the weather station so that Joanne wouldn't get behind on her physical science project.

Once Bette was struggling with writing a paper. Christa read it and said, "You can't turn this in like it is!" She edited the paper, corrected the spelling and sentence structure, and typed it. Bette received a C over F: the F because her subject was not acceptable, and a C because the paper read well and was typed.

The three friends spent weekends skiing at Pat's Peak in Henniker, New Hampshire. The first time they went, Joanne's car broke down on Route 89, just outside of Bow. It was pitch dark. They looked at the motor with a flashlight but couldn't tell what was wrong.

Christa volunteered to go with the first motorist who would stop, and to find a garage to help them. A red car pulled up and a young blond fellow offered a ride. Christa jumped in, leaving Bette and Joanne with the car. "I'll be back with a tow truck," she shouted. A half-hour passed, then an hour, and then Bette and Joanne began to panic. They heard a radio news flash that a male inmate had escaped from the Concord prison and stolen a *red* car. The police were cautioning residents to lock their doors because he was dangerous. Bette and Joanne became almost hysterical with worry. They locked up the car and, taking the flashlight, started walking in hopes of finding help. It was freezing, and no cars came by.

Then out of the darkness came flashing yellow lights and big head-lights. There was Christa riding in the cab of a huge tow truck. As Bette and Joanne, with tear-streaked faces, climbed into the warm cab, they explained why they were so upset. Christa told them she was so late because they couldn't find any garage still open. The young man then drove to his hometown, where he roused the local garage owner from his dinner. This mechanic was glad to help. He hitched the little car to the tow bar, drove back to the garage, replaced the fan belt, and sent them on their way.

In spite of that beginning, they had a great time skiing and went back often. Once they brought back a "frost heaves" sign that they picked up from the side of the road. They had never seen a sign like that before, nor had they ever heard of the frost heaves warning that lets New Hampshire motorists know that the roadway may be buckled or bumpy because of extreme cold and thaw.

Joanne made many trips to Virginia Military Institute with Christa to visit Steve McAuliffe. One such trip was Joanne's first plane ride, and she sat clutching Christa's hand all the way. Christa showed her Washington, D.C., between plane and bus connections. They toured the museums and galleries, and both did very well in their art history classes because of their visits to the National Gallery.

Joanne remembers Christa as being so much more adventuresome than she, always on the lookout for ethnic foods and striking up a con-versation with anyone nearby. Christa could be at home whether she was sitting in on a court session or sitting in a grubby bus depot.

Christa put up with Joanne's love of nature. They would often pull the car off the road to get a look at plants unknown to New England. They explored backroads and battlefields, and searched for arrowheads, musket balls, and old stone walls.

On one of the trips to VMI, they found that Steve had pulled guard duty. Christa spent the time walking back and forth with him, gabbing. Once they picked Steve up from summer training camp in Pennsylvania and went exploring the "Dutch" country. There Joanne took a picture of them standing in front of a Conestoga wagon, holding hands. Joanne said that it seemed as if Christa belonged there, ready to drive that wagon across the prairies on to new lands and adventures.

Bette, Joanne, and Christa had many intense discussions about the Vietnam War. Steve, whose father was a retired career U.S. Army man, had also chosen to begin a military career. Christa – like many Americans in the sixties – had ambivalent feelings about the war. Her support for the military conflicted with doubts about the wisdom of the mission that they had been given in Vietnam. Christa and her friends opposed Communism, but they were horrified at the killings. Both Bette and Joanne were close to young men who opposed the war, and who claimed they would rather move to Canada than serve if called up by the draft.

During their last years at college, Bette and Joanne worked toward their certification to teach elementary school, and Christa worked toward a history major with a minor in education.

Retired professor Carolla Hagland said, "Christa had something special. You remember the very good students." Professor Hagland's history course, The American Frontier, was based on readings from the journals of frontiersmen and women, and it inspired Christa to keep a journal of her own.

"Christa majored in history yet she was chosen to be part of a very scientific program," said retired Framingham State College professor Joseph Boothroyd, who trained her as a student teacher. "She showed that by getting a good liberal arts education you learn how to live and not just how to make a living. Christa McAuliffe was successful in all her endeavors because she knew how to live." Christa finished her studies with good grades, but she had to work hard for them; they didn't come easily.

With the help of her adviser, Christa entered an honors program and chose anti-Semitism as the topic for her thesis. Besides her research, she battered Bette with all kinds of questions about the high holy days, the holocaust survivors, what it was like being a Cantor (Bette's dad was a Cantor), and whether Bette had experienced any anti-Semitism growing up.

Later, when Joanne was planning her wedding, Christa had Joanne try on her wedding dress. It fit just fine, and Christa insisted that Joanne wear it. Joanne's wedding pictures are a reminder that Christa was not only generous but pragmatic, too.

Then in 1986, the college friends were at Cape Canaveral. Bette and her dad flew to Florida for the launch, and Joanne, her husband, Rick Brown, their three daughters, Rick's parents, and Joanne's dad all drove down in their van to see "our Christa," as Joanne's kids called her.

A teachers' convention was being held at Cape Canaveral in the days before the scheduled liftoff. The science experiments that Christa would conduct in space were explained, and teachers were taken on special tours at the Kennedy Space Center. The huge shuttle assembly plant was opened up so that they could see where the shuttle was lodged before it was taken to the launch pad. Teachers exchanged pins, attended lecture series, listened to astronauts speak, and met the eight Teacher-in-Space finalists.

Joanne and Rick left the reception that we hosted for Christa's friends and family and found the pipes in their hotel room had frozen from the cold weather. Joanne had a strong premonition and became so upset that they packed up the van and left for home. In Georgia, they pulled over to the side of the road to watch as the shuttle lifted off.

Then they drove straight through until they reached home. When Joanne went to the nursery school where she taught, she discovered that the children thought she had died from pieces of the shuttle hitting her on the head. Some of the children thought that everyone watching the launch was killed by the shuttle falling.

Also after Christa's reception, Bette and her dad were walking on the outside terrace of their hotel when Bette's purse was snatched from her arm. The pull made her lose her balance and wrench her ankle. She was in pain, and was so upset that they left for home the next day.

Bette arrived in New Hampshire on Monday and went to her school Tuesday. Her second graders were watching the liftoff on a small black-and-white television in their classroom. Bette switched off the set as the malfunction occurred. A precocious child said, "It didn't look right, Miss Chase." Bette locked herself in the bathroom.

Christa and Steven

Christa met Steve McAuliffe during her sophomore year at Marian High School in Framingham. From that time on, they were a couple. After graduation in June 1966, Steve went to Virginia Military Institute, and

Christa stayed at home, attending Framingham State College as a day student. Steve would be home some holidays, and Christa would go to Virginia for dances and special events.

One Friday when she was planning to take a flight to Virginia for the weekend, it started to snow. By afternoon, the snowfall was becoming heavy. Christa came in from classes worried that the airport would shut down, and sure enough, it did. She called Steve, and they commiserated over the phone.

The snow started to taper off and stopped around six o'clock. The airport reopened, so we waited for Ed to get home from work and give us a report on the road conditions. When he came in, he said, "O.K., let's give it a try." Christa jumped up and threw her arms around him, and off they went.

Once she was airborne, I was to call Steve and let him know she was coming. Of course, by that time I was unable to reach him because the cadets were at the dance, so I did the next best thing and left a message.

That evening we were at a house party, and I began to worry whether Christa had arrived safely. Steve wasn't expecting her. How would he know she was coming? Why hadn't I thought to have her call us? All kinds of thoughts went through my head – anything could have happened! I spent the evening calling the school, trying to get a message through to the dance. Finally, one did get through, and I soon learned that Christa had arrived and met a surprised and delighted Steve.

Virginia Military Institute graduates were required to give four years of service to the Army after graduation. Steve received special permission to attend law school before entering the service. After graduating from VMI in 1970, Steve planned to attend Georgetown University's Law School that fall. (Later, after graduation from Georgetown, he completed his military service with the army's legal services branch.) When they learned that Steve had been accepted by Georgetown, Christa and Steve made plans to marry.

The wedding date was set for August 23, 1970, and Steve had to report to class on August 25. We had six weeks for planning, and everything fell neatly into place. Christa wanted to make her own wedding dress, so she and Anne Donovan, who had been her friend since the fifth grade and was to be her maid of honor, went looking to see what style would be best. Within an hour they came flying into the house. "We found exactly what I want," called Christa, "right size and all!" Back out they went, I with them, and I did agree that the dress was perfect. It was lace with beautiful simple lines. So instead of making her dress, she bought that one. We found a dress that we liked for Anne and ordered the same material to make the gowns for the three junior bridesmaids: twelve-year-old Lisa, eleven-year-old Betsy, and Steve's twelve-year-old sister Melissa. Christa ran into a bit of trouble fitting the girls' youthful figures. Fortunately, an excellent seamstress worked in Ed's office and offered to help. Muffy Higgins's talent saved the day, and the dresses looked beautiful on the girls.

Christa and Steve planned their wedding with her cousin, Father Jim Leary. They wrote part of the ceremony and intended to say their vows facing the congregation. As music, they wanted "A Time for Us," the theme song from the movie *Romeo and Juliet*. The wedding was scheduled for five o'clock on a Sunday afternoon at St. Jeremiah's Church. The reception was to be held at our home immediately after the ceremony.

On Saturday, a large yellow and white striped tent was set up in our backyard and the poles decorated with greens. Tables and chairs were put in place, and the band would be set up in one corner. The caterer's work area was partitioned off in the garage, and champagne was chilling in a large tub. Everything seemed ready. The caterers would see to the linens and the flowers the next day.

Our garden and patio looked lovely, bright with orange and yellow flowers. When we later met one of Christa's friends in Maryland, she said she was so impressed when Christa told her that the garden flowers complemented the bridesmaids' gowns.

Just before it was time to dress and leave for the wedding rehearsal, I went over the grounds carefully, plucking off any dead or dying flowers and then gave all the plants a thorough watering. It was becoming late, so I left the hose curled up on the lawn to be put away later.

The next morning, we woke to the sound of rain, hard rain coming down in sheets. Christa opened one eye and pulled the covers over her head. I hoped for a break in the deluge to take care of the hose that I could just about see through the curtain of rain.

Two men came to reinforce the sides of the tent with extra canvas and to tighten the ropes because the top was sagging with the water weight. A neighbor called to tell Christa that rain was a good omen – it meant a happy marriage, and that certainly proved to be true. The hairdresser came in dripping. The rain wouldn't let up. It was impossible to go out and not become wet, no matter what protection you had. I was afraid that the ground would be soaked beneath the tent – where could one find 200 pairs of rubbers for their guests? But the ground was fine – the reinforcement held.

Father Leary was to concelebrate the nuptial mass with Father Gerald Corrigan, another cousin who had officiated at Ed's and my wedding in 1947; Monsignor William Shea, chaplain of Marian High School; Father Joseph McCall, our pastor; and Father Daniel Quinn, assistant pastor.

Everyone was waiting at the church. Shortly after five, the downpour began to subside. As the sun gleamed through the stained glass windows, Father McCall announced, "Our bride will be here shortly; the rain has stopped for her, and the sun is shining."

And the bride *was* beautiful as she walked down the aisle on her father's arm, her smile radiant. Christa carried my white prayer book, given to me for my wedding day by my Aunt Frances.

Christa and Steve left about eleven o'clock that night to drive to Sturbridge, Massachusetts, and then to go on to Maryland the next day. Later Christa wrote us about their evening after leaving home. "The Publick House at Sturbridge was really nice – all antique. They even had lemon soap and two apples on our bureau." It wasn't until much later that Christa confided in us that when they tried to check in at Sturbridge, their reservations were missing. They had already paid for their room, but since they didn't have a receipt with them, they had to re-register and pay again. At that point they were tired, and it was nearly midnight. They were just happy to be able to have a place to stay for the night. Christa ended her letter with, "I miss you all, naturally, but I am really happy. The wedding was so beautiful. We can't wait to see how the pictures came out."

III

Family and Career:
1970s-1980s

Getting Settled in Maryland

On August 28, 1970, five days after the wedding, Christa wrote and described her apartment in Maryland, saying that they had almost everything out of boxes.

We went down to VMI and picked up Steve's and Wayne's [Steve's brother] "racks," otherwise known as beds. Both mattresses fit in a double fitted sheet when the racks are pushed together – so far, they haven't moved!

We are using the tray tables – two pushed together with a tablecloth over them – for our dining room table.

Steve is busy already – just orientation, and already he has assignments. I'm going to a lecture with him tomorrow. Ralph Nader is speaking.

The Georgetown section is beautiful. It has all these little shops, and the university is huge, its buildings are stone.

The gas stove and oven are going to take some getting used to, but today I baked chicken and muffins, and everything came out fine.

We went looking for furniture yesterday. There are a lot of sales on now for unfinished furniture. We need a desk and some bookcases. But I wish you could see it now – it really looks great. I mean considering not having any furniture.

Steve and I went to an outdoor ballet last night by the Washington monument. It was beautiful and the costuming was so colorful. We went over to the Lincoln Memorial afterwards – this is so impressive at night. Tell Stephen and Kit good luck at school and DON'T GET BEHIND on your assignments, especially the first month.

The next day another note came: "I forgot to tell you that the stereo you gave us was the first thing we unpacked! The FM stations here are really good, too. I wish you could hear the tone. It's just fabulous."

On August 30, she wrote about swimming in their apartment complex's olympic-size pool: "It's beautiful. And it's warm down here. I think I prefer New England weather. This weather and accent take a while to get used to. We are going to invest in a fan." They had also found a church: "It is really small but close by on Pennsylvania Avenue going into D.C., and it does have air conditioning!"

There were changes for Ed and me also – Stephen left for his first year at Colgate University in Hamilton, New York, a week after Christa was married. He had to report in early because he was playing football. A week after that, Kit was to be at Post Junior College in Waterbury, Connecticut. Before this, none of our children had lived away from home. Then within three weeks, three of them were gone. It was strange to shrink from a family of seven to a family of four so suddenly. Strange it was, but sort of peaceful and quiet. But that didn't last long! Before we got a chance to get used to the calm, it was time to plan for Thanksgiving.

Christa wrote on September 9 that she had made the rounds of six schools in the immediate area applying for a position as a substitute teacher, and that she had a job for Thursday. The principal told her to come in after she had substituted to tell him how it went and how she liked it, because he thought that he might have a permanent position opening up. That fall, Christa began her teaching career in the Prince Georges County Schools at Benjamin Foulois Junior High School in Morningside, Maryland. The school was only ten minutes from Christa and Steve's apartment.

In the same letter she said that they had gone to a Goodwill store on Saturday and bought a huge desk and a round dining table. They were going to refinish both. She wrote:

Steve painted the kitchen cabinets bright yellow and I made orange and yellow flowered curtains. Everything is so nice and bright.

Steve got a non-paying job with the Legal Aid Society. It's kind of hard to get into, but fortunately a third-year student that Steve met at Indiantown Gap Summer Camp had some pull. He had to be sworn in, and he works as an investigator under an attorney whom he is going to meet today. He does get ten cents a mile for traveling when he's investigating. It sounds really interesting, and he's all excited about it.

Bob Blair [an usher at their wedding from Hawaii] arrived last night. I think he'll be staying here for a few days. He doesn't have to be at school until September 17.

October 3: "We visited Bob for a couple of days at the University of North Carolina. The school is beautiful – a huge campus with gorgeous buildings. Bob's not too happy with the law school. He liked what he saw at Georgetown. His dorm is co-ed, so Steve and I stayed in Bob's room, and he used another room for the weekend."

October 5: "Teaching is a lot better than an office job, but I can't elaborate on the joys of teaching as yet! Some of my classes are great, but there are a few kids that disrupt the rest. One kid in particular I'm ready to string up! But it's still early, and I've much to learn about control – so I'll give you a mid-year report in January!"

By the end of October, Christa was disgusted and felt that school was a

total waste of time as far as school work goes. Eighth grade testing took place for three days, which meant that I was left with anywhere from five to fifteen kids in my classes. So, I couldn't give any new material or start another unit. And the annual candy sale started Monday, so each day we have lost an entire period as the "candy aides" distribute the boxes to the students.

We had an unpleasant experience: this morning we discovered that both snow tires had been stolen from the trunk of our car. The car had been locked and the vent window pried open and the catch broken since the trunk lever is in the glove compartment. All the way to school we talked about moving, but when I was telling one of the history teachers what happened, she said it had happened to her twice and her apartment is in an expensive project. We called the insurance company and picked up two new tires. I guess we will have to take them in each night with us!

I found great recipes – pork chops stuffed with mushrooms and cheese, stuffed cucumbers, and barbecued spare ribs with sweet-sour sauce. After a week of soup and hot dogs, Steve and I are eating well again. Actually, we didn't mind at all.

Steve spent all last night planning the construction of a room divider. We are getting the lumber this week. I have no space – counter space – in the kitchen, so Steve's going to build shelves in there, too. The carpenter-lawyer!

He spent the entire day in court – the trial for the lawyer he's working for came up, and he wanted to see how it came out. He learns more criminal justice in court rather than in class."

November: "The kids at school have calmed down, but there are still a few I would like to string up. My seventh period class is a zoo. I found out through the faculty lounge that I have the largest class load in the school, outside of the gym instructors – great!"

February: "The administration won't back you up on discipline. In fact, the latest is you talk to the parents when a kid is suspended. Now, I wouldn't mind if we regulated the suspensions, but the office suspends the kids and you get to straighten out everything with the parents. I felt like a fool sitting there talking to two parents (the kid got into a fight in my class). I had no idea what the precedent was – it was ridiculous."

February brought a visit from her Framingham State College friends Bette Chase and Joanne Connor. Christa was delighted to have them with her for a few days. And February also brought snow to the ski areas:

The skiing last week was beautiful – they have two double chair lifts and the trails are long and rather gentle . . . We went skiing with five other members of the faculty and had a real good time. I was exhausted Friday, and Steve slept all day, but it was worth it. There was about seven inches of new snow on the ground, and it wasn't crowded at all. We are thinking of going up next week and staying overnight to get a couple of days of skiing in.

I'm being real brave and probably insane, but I'm taking 55 kids on a field trip March 15 into the FBI building. Another teacher is going with me, and it doesn't look too bad – yet! Of course, I'm taking two of my better classes – there are two classes I wouldn't even take to another classroom.

I have a student teacher in my room observing for a couple of days. She still wanted to teach after seeing the classes, so I must be doing something right. Actually, the kids weren't really awful that day, so at least on the surface things looked good. She did say that her brother loved the class (I have him fifth period), so maybe I'm reaching someone.

In March she wrote:

The Maryland legislature has a bill before it to abolish the principal's right to suspend students from school. This system is so lax on discipline – I really can't believe that they'd take away the only recourse open to getting rid of problem students. You sign a contract to *teach* yet end up doing everything but that. The students who want to learn and the teachers who want to teach are hindered by compulsory education which insists that students who don't want to go to school have to. In one class, I have two kids who cause so much trouble and pass in no work, and I have no action from their parents, guidance, or the administration. But when things get too unbearable, one is suspended, and I have rest for a few days at least. If you remove the threat of suspension, which does subdue some students, you open the doors to chaos. There are enough obstacles in the way of the teaching-learning process as it is. Why add more? The county system is really poorly run – so many "law wives" I have talked to have left Prince Georges for the same reasons I'm complaining about. One girl was a fourth grade teacher who was attacked six times by her students, and nothing was done. Another teaching eighth grade math was threatened with obscene notes and letters when she gave failure notices! Problems of education.

Christa at three months.

Carson's Beach, Dorchester,
where we lived in the summer
of 1950: Christa, Grace, and Teddy.

Ed's graduation 1951, Boston College.
Stella Corrigan, Ed Corrigan,
Christa, James Corrigan.

Christa at two years.

Christa at four years.

Easter 1954, at Brookfield Circle
(our first Framingham home):
Kit, Christa, Steve.

First Communion, 1956.

Brook Water School, fifth-grade portrait.

To
Mommy
~
Daddy

Christa Corrigan

Christmas 1960, Brookfield Circle:
Kit, Christa with Betsy, Steve, Lisa (in
foreground).

Confirmation, St. Jeremiah's Church, 1961:
Betsy, Christa, Ed, Lisa.

Christmas 1961, Joseph Road, Framingham:
Steve, Kit, Betsy, Christa, Lisa.

Christa at sixteen.

Sound of Music intermission, 1966: Christa plays the vibraphone in her nun's costume.

Christa's Girl Scout troop at home, 1967.

Did I tell you I'm taking 188 kids to Gettysburg, Pennsylvania? They should have fun – it's an all-day trip.

Christa railed against the endless forms to fill out, pupil personality cards, CRI forms, CRZ forms, a bureaucratic mess. In between all of this one is supposed to be teaching? "They have final exams of two hours in length, given as busy work for the kids so teachers can get their paper work done. General consensus is no one corrects them, but the copies have to be on file in the office – what a waste!"

Disillusionment came when two classes were acting up, with some kids answering back and talking through classes. "Had five parent conferences with no results – they can't seem to get it through their heads that they are here to learn. After spending three weeks of preparing the unit, it becomes utter chaos. They are so used to being spoon fed, given both the questions and the answers to study for 'programmed learning.' Imagine what their first essay questions will be like!"

She wrote on March 24:

Steve and I had a busy weekend. Around 7:00 on Friday, we went to Quantico Marine Base in Virginia. It turned out to be a regular VMI reunion since four or five of Steve's friends were there. We didn't get in until 3:30 a.m.

On Saturday, I went into Georgetown to do some shopping, and Steve had to sit in on a jury for a moot court trial held at the Federal Court Building, which lasted until 5:30. After lunch, I sat in court. The trial was really boring. The students were spending so much time on trivial points – probably to get a better grade. There was an actual Federal Court judge there "donating" his time to Georgetown Law Center. That night, we went to a surprise birthday party for one of Steve's friends. By 10:00, we felt as though it were 2:00 in the morning!

I'm so glad the weather is getting nice. I can't wait for the cherry blossoms! Every year I've been down here in April, and each year I've missed them. It's even light when I leave for school in the morning!

In May, Christa found out that the school system had no position for her in the next school year, 1971–72:

The kids at school are so funny. Some asked me if I was coming back next year. I tried to explain that I was "laid off," but the next day I found a group furtively signing a petition against having me fired! I explained again, but I actually don't think it got through.

Another Monday, but only four weeks left and neither of us has a summer job yet! I better start calling the places where I've applied. Steve went up to Capitol Hill and talked to a few representatives about possible jobs and has applied to about 20 governmental agencies. He probably won't have any problem getting work, but I hope he gets something where he can use his legal knowledge.

The weekend here was rainy – not very good weather to go anywhere. So I spent the time sewing and Steve studying. He called Jack Sheedy in New Jersey last night, and over the Memorial Day weekend we are going with Jack and Judy to New York to see Mike and Leslie Shew. So that's something to look forward to, especially since Steve will be finished with exams by then.

Did I tell you I'm playing a game with my first period class? It's a foreign policy simulation game called *Dangerous Parallel*. It simulates the world crisis during the outbreak of the Korean War. I'm using my top group, and it's working out well. Each set of six students takes a fictional country, and they delegate responsibilities through the chief minister – all students have a part (as finance minister, ambassador-at-large, etc.). The object of the game is to make decisions according to the goals you have set up for your country. A filmstrip is shown illustrating one country invading the other and how the other countries reacted. The crisis is stated and the student groups react. It's really fascinating! They can make world statements via telstar satellite. All have badges to wear so when they negotiate, everyone will know who they are. The kids are having a great time, and so am I. It's nice seeing them enthusiastically get into class and into their groups – ready to make decisions.

I'm starting a game called *Ghetto* in seventh period today. I hope it works! These kids are lazy, apathetic brats who don't react to much – however, perhaps there is hope that this will kindle some interest.

Later she wrote:

We are playing *Ghetto,* and boy is it tiring – I never get a chance to sit down and catch my breath. But the kids are having fun and have really been enthusiastic about the game.

I had another run-in with the administration. They wanted us to give a mark – final grades for kids who are failing – last week! This is without their makeup work or final exam grade! I really didn't know in a couple of cases, and we had to abide by the mark. Anyway, after a half hour of deciding who was failing in the eighth grade (they would have to stay back unless they attended summer school), the principal tells me fifteen kids are too many to fail, and they couldn't have that so he changed some of the grades. Everyone was boiling! Can you imagine – the kids do *nothing* to get passed, not even makeup work! What a way to run a school!

We have a school faculty dinner June 10 for the end of the year. Just about everyone is going, and it will be nice to keep in touch with people during the summer.

Steve and I are chaperoning a group of ninth graders June 12 to the beach for the day. It sounds like fun!

In July, Christa went to visit the school where she would be teaching in the fall of 1971 – Thomas Johnson Middle School in Bowie, Maryland. She met her department head and got her books. He told her that one of the school's problems was that it drew kids from two neighborhoods: one with expensive homes and the other, welfare recipients. He also let it be known that he had had problems the previous year with the English department's "stealing" his subject areas – like ecology and pollution. "Since I'll be teaching three classes in each area," Christa wrote, "I guess I'll be hearing complaints from both sides." She would teach at this school until she and Steve moved to New Hampshire in 1978.

That summer, Steve and Christa enjoyed short getaways. They rented bikes at Fletcher's Boathouse and went riding along the C&O Canal. "To get to the boathouse, we had to ferry ourselves over using a rowboat and pulley. The bike trail is 100 miles long. Needless to say, we only went out one hour and then came back. The ride was tiring though. My knees were shaking when we turned our bikes in. The bicycle path is right next to the canal – it proved hazardous for a group of Boy Scouts when their leader fell in! He was all right though. There are picnic benches in places, and we stopped for lunch. It's a nice place to spend the day."

Christa and Steve went to an open-air concert in the new planned community of Columbus, Maryland. Robert Merrill sang with the National Symphony at the Merriweather Post Pavilion. Christa reported:

We enjoyed the concert, especially the selections from *Carmen*. Columbus is unbelievable – the housing is gorgeous and, of course, the concept of a planned community is beautiful.

We went out to eat crabs the other week, and Steve wants to go again. He must have eaten about twenty-five! They gave us huge platters of deep fried oysters – they were delicious. Even Steve the oyster-hater ate them.

Steve has attended some of the concerned officers meetings. I was able to go with him to hear Eugene McCarthy and Senator Groening. Groening is remarkable, a sharp wit and tremendous speaker – and he's 85! The Senator was also one of the first "doves" who opposed the Gulf of Tonkin Resolution. McCarthy, naturally, was playing politician and really didn't answer any questions directly. He's very impressive, though.

That November we read:

I can't believe this 80-degree weather on November 2! Foolishly, I packed all my summer clothes away, and, naturally, the heat is on in school. The kids are falling asleep in classes because the room is so warm. And tomorrow is supposed to be just as warm.

We didn't get many kids on Saturday night [for Halloween]. Steve carved out our pumpkin. We put it on the shelf in the back room and turned off the lights. When the kids came into the room, it really looked eerie!

I decided to cook a nice dinner Monday. Shrimp cocktail, beef in beer, green beans and almonds, tabbouleh, and Steve's favorite dessert, Boston creme pie. I had everything ready, and the pilot light went out on the stove! I finally got the top to light, but the oven had to be fixed by maintenance, and naturally, they didn't come until Tuesday. Well, the dinner came off fine – but no dessert!

With all the activity at school and meetings, I've been getting home around 4:00 and have to battle commuter traffic. Today I better leave at 3:00 since I'm meeting Steve so I can attend one of his classes. He loves tax law and has been raving about this particular professor.

A follow-up letter indicated:

Friday at last! Steve's tax class was great. I can see why he likes it since the man is so interesting. He really makes tax come alive.

I assigned projects from my three history classes and all 109 of them came in yesterday. Will I ever learn? Some are very good though. One girl wove with yarn the ceremonial headdresses worn by the Indians.

A pay raise was retracted, and Christa wrote that what was really annoying about it was that most of the teachers had already spent it. She was having an extra $25 taken out of each week's salary to help pay the rising Georgetown tuition, but now that would have to be canceled.

It was during this period, as Christa was getting her feet wet in teaching and feeling her way forward, that she decided to earn her Master of Arts degree in secondary school administration and supervision in hopes that she might obtain a better position and have some power to bring about changes in the educational system. She enrolled in the necessary courses at Bowie State College, and her M.Ed. degree was conferred in January 1978.

Earlier, in 1972, she wrote:

> Steve is full of ambition, started running 1.3 miles each day, and went on a diet. He is also giving me my anniversary present starting yesterday – he's going to do all the housework and cook for a week. I enjoyed sitting back while he folded the laundry and set the table! And he's cooking dinner, too. He's also letting the girls in the office at the law school know what he's doing so that their husbands will be "working," too.
>
> School's keeping me busy during the week – the school partnership in Liberia, the yearbook, the career workshop that we are setting up for the kids in February where people of all sorts of professions are coming to speak. I've also been learning how to develop film – I did two rolls last week and even enlarged some 8 × 10's. It's lots of fun. Oh, yes, and in between all this I'm teaching a unit on consumer law.

That April, Christa became involved with curriculum change in the county. "In fact," she wrote, "I have six meetings coming up on writing a pretest in social studies skills, and I'm being paid $50 a day. The law-related education has a good chance of being approved, and I'm in that course. I'll be paid for teaching a course to teachers in the fall. So beyond being just interesting, I'll get some compensation."

Flowers – Like Mother, Like Daughter

I clip coupons, take advantage of bargains, have a compost pile, use strips of newspaper to edge my gardens, and wash plastic bags. I can't stand waste. Leftover vegetables make a great soup, soft fruits a just-right sauce, and trifle needs some day-old cake. One day Christa was folding her laundry when one of her friends stopped by to visit.

"Why in the world do you wash plastic bags?" the friend asked.

Christa shrugged and answered, "I don't know, my Mother does it."

Sometimes, seeing your child do things just as you do them brings a great sense of pleasure and accomplishment. As Ed and I drove home from one of our visits with Christa and Steve, we talked about how happy they were and how cozy they had made their apartment. We were proud that they knew how to relax and escape pressure.

Ed commented, "I couldn't help but notice how Christa does so many things the same way you do. Did you notice the philodendron on the top of the china cabinet? The leaves are hanging down the side – the same as ours at home." It does make one stop and think how our children mimic us, and most of the time, I'm sure it is done subconsciously.

When they were first settling in Maryland, Christa and Steve went for a walk and brought back to their apartment dried flowers and weeds. "I made a couple of dried bouquets," she wrote. "They look sharp."

Christa did enjoy her plants, and she would write about them in her letters: "We have a split-leaf philodendron in the living room in a huge brown ceramic earthenware pot. I bought leaf polish for the leaves. Do philodendrons need much sunlight?" In another letter she commented: "The amber bowl we got for a wedding present is beautiful with flowers. I have violet mums in it now, and it adds so much to the room." That spring they bought a large rubber plant for the kitchen. "Do they need much water? It only gets about an hour of sunlight a day – is that enough? And what type of soil do you use? I bought potting soil for my little plant and philodendron soil for my split-leaf, but both pots get like clay and the soil cakes and gets hard. I break it up every day, but it seems as if there should be a better way."

In July 1971, Christa wrote about visiting the National Botanical Gardens.

I had often wanted to go but never seemed to make the trip. I got there around 1:00 and didn't leave until almost 4:00. The gardens are spectacular. There are different rooms set at a certain temperature and humidity for "ideal" growing conditions. As you walk in, there are long goldfish ponds and tropical plants. Some of the leaves are four to five feet long and three feet wide! The ferns are huge – some reaching up to ten feet. You feel as if you are in the land of the giants. They had elephant ear plants that had 30 to 40 four-foot leaves on them.

They also have the most beautiful orchids. There are about 50 plants in bloom. Some flowers were only an inch; others were huge. One of the gardeners was telling me that there were 2500 varieties and the orchid is the most common flower in the world. He told me which ones had scent. You couldn't touch, but you could sniff. I could have stayed there all day just looking at them.

One room had nothing but cactus in it – huge plants, ten to twenty feet tall.

And they only blossom at night. Some had large buds on them. The varieties were endless. Of course, they have collected plants from all over the world. Some tiny flowers were out – paper thin petals and no stem. They seemed just to grow out of the cactus.

It was a tremendous experience – when you come down we'll have to go there. The gardener said they have greenhouses that furnish most of the flowering plants. He comes every day and changes the orchids. The "best time" for viewing many different varieties is January. I'll have to go back then.

I found out the name of the plant Kit gave you. They have quite a few varieties of it at the gardens. It's a spathephyllum clevelandii, and it comes from Mexico. There is also a neat ground cover here called "baby tears" – tiny leaves, pale green. It was gorgeous. There is also a fingernail plant from Brazil – long shiny leaves with a half circle of red at the end! Their colors were beautiful – pinks and reds with rippled edges. The gardener must have been impressed since I was there so long, so he took me on a "personal" tour and then surreptitiously snipped some clippings of cacti and a couple of little plants and put them into a paper bag for me. The plants are a type of African violet and have (or will have) bright red-orange flowers. I can't remember the names of the cacti, but he told me to let the ends of the cuttings dry out completely and then just pop them into some sand and roots will grow. He showed me some cacti he was rooting. He had been there for years and knows so much about plants. Only four gardeners and two "bosses" take care of the gardens, and they are beautifully kept. I'm so pleased with the little plants. I hope they flower soon. When I come home, I'll bring you a cutting.

The next time we visited, Christa took us to the Botanical Gardens, sought out the gardener who befriended her, and introduced us. She also gave him a report on the condition of the cuttings he had given her.

One day I called Christa, and the phone rang so long that I was about to hang up when she answered, out of breath. She and her friend Sue Rowold had been out picking grapes to make jelly. She was outside the apartment when she heard the phone ringing. Her arms were filled with brown paper bags piled high with grapes, and in her hurry to answer the phone, she dropped the bags while struggling through the door. Grapes spilled out everywhere, inside and outside the apartment, scattering through the living room and rolling down the hallway. "You should see this mess I'm in! Grapes are everywhere!" With that picture in mind, I started to giggle, then we both had a good laugh.

In early 1974 Christa and Steve moved from their apartment to a home in Oxon Hill, Maryland, a split-level with a lovely yard. In the backyard and on the side were two huge rose bushes that needed attention. They were scraggly and too long, but after being cut and tied to a trellis, they looked attractive. The yard also had azaleas, forsythia, and lilacs. Christa planted bulbs.

Early that spring, she watched the green shoots popping from the ground. She wrote, "I'm hoping we won't have too much more cold weather. It did snow and get cold, but the tops of the plants didn't freeze, so I guess they'll be okay. They should look gorgeous."

That March, she and Sue planned to have vegetable gardens. "We first thought of having just one large one at Sue's place so we both could work on it, but I'd like the convenience of having my own, so we decided to each have tomatoes and lettuce, but we would divide the rest of the crops so we'd get a good variety. I'll plant eggplant, broccoli, radishes, and a few other vegetables. Sue will plant other varieties. We have great hopes for freezing many vegetables for the winter. We are also going to make jellies and jams – I finally found a store that has canning supplies. I'd like to get some marmalade made before Easter – I'll bring some up for Grandma."

In April, they had an unusual storm and wondered if we had one also; electricity was out for days, they lost shingles from the roof, and there were quite a few broken branches around. "The flowers were beaten to death. Fortunately, the tulips weren't blooming. That would have made me mad. The daffodils are still coming up, but I'm afraid the crocuses have had it."

In June, a stretch of hot, humid weather made everyone anxious for the school year to end. "The yard looks so nice," Christa reported, "I think you spurred us on with all that work you did for us while you were down. The garden is going strong – beans, peas, and tomatoes in flower. We've had loads of radishes and lettuce. Steve's corn is really growing. He is so excited about it. An angel trumpet bloomed! I just love having a garden."

When Christa and Steve moved to Concord, New Hampshire, in 1978, they did not have room for a large vegetable garden. The town allotted gardening space for residents, so Christa got together with friends and had a thriving vegetable garden. They took turns going out to water and harvest. She not only enjoyed working in the soil, but also doing the preserving. We all received gifts of her jams, jellies, relishes, and pickles, and her pumpkin and zucchini breads.

At Christa's memorial service, Steve had huge baskets of white mums placed on the altar. The only other flowers were from President and Mrs. Reagan – a red, white, and blue wreath. All other floral arrangements were sent to hospitals, nursing homes, and other churches.

That spring, President and Mrs. Reagan sent a stunning bouquet of flowers in various shades of blue and violet arranged in a tall oval brown ceramic vase. After a few days, they needed some attention. I was freshening the water and removing a few drooping leaves when Christa's friend Jo Ann Jordan stopped in to visit. She commented on how beautiful the flowers were and asked if I had arranged them.

"Oh no," I answered, "these came from the president."

Jo Ann's eyes widened. "The president? You mean *the* president?"

When I answered yes, we looked at each other and burst out laughing. "Can't you just imagine Christa saying, 'Now *really!*'?"

Generosity – A Hallmark

Steve McAuliffe's birthday is March 3, and mine is March 4. Just as we used to jointly celebrate the children's birthdays, Christa's birthday, and Christa and Steve's anniversary together in late August or early September, Steve and I would celebrate our March birthdays together. One year when we held the birthday party at our home in Framingham, I found that Steve and Christa's present to me was an airplane lesson – a flying lesson! I really became so excited: in the first place, it was an absolute surprise, and in the second place, it was something I had always wanted to do but never thought I would.

The lesson was scheduled for a short time later. Ed and I went up to Concord, as Christa and Steve had made arrangements for me to take my flying lesson at Concord Airport. The morning we started off to the airport, Ed elected to stay at Christa's; he said he and Scott would be at home hiding under the bed as the plane came zooming by the house. That's how much confidence they had in me!

Christa and Steve and I went to the airport and met the instructor; he and I hopped into the little Cessna and waved good-bye to the two of them. The instructor first showed me what to do with my feet. He said

59

that you steer with your feet, which was completely new to me. As I was working the pedals he said, "Now you see this line down the runway? Follow that line and you are going to be steering." So as I worked the completely unfamiliar pedals, we kind of zigzagged down the runway. Then the instructor told me pull up on the steering wheel of the plane. Of course, when I did that, we took off up into the sky. How exciting that was! It was especially exciting to me because he was actually letting me fly the plane. He was there with his own instruments, but he was letting me do the flying. We banked around, and he explained all the instruments on the panels. I was trying to listen although it seemed impossible to understand anything. But it was wonderful to be up in the sky! It was a beautiful day, and the sky was nice and clear. The instructor was showing me how to bank and how to turn. As we were going along, he said, "Now there is one thing you always have to watch out for, and that, of course, is make sure there are no other planes around you." As soon as I heard that, I whipped my head around to the left and right and up and down searching the sky for planes, and consequently the airplane was zooming all around while I was doing this – dipping and turning. All too soon the half-hour in the air was over, and we headed back. The instructor took the plane down, showing me how to do it. We taxied down the runway to where Christa and Steve were waiting. When we stepped out of the plane, I was so excited – I had loved every minute! I rushed over to Christa and Steve, who asked, "Well, how did you like it?"

"Oh, I loved it, loved it, loved it!" I exclaimed. "Did you know that I was the one that taxied down the runway and took off?"

Steve looked at me, and then he and Christa looked at each other as they said, "Yeah, we could tell!" Then it was time to go back to the house and get Ed and Scott from under the bed and tell them that it was safe to come out.

Christa and Steve were always generous. They helped with everything along the way when they possibly could – even for their wedding. After they went to listen to the band that was going to play, Christa and Steve decided that we had enough expense as it was, and they were going to hire the band – which they did.

When they were still living in their second apartment in Maryland, Ed and I received a special-delivery letter. With the letter was a pair of round-trip airline tickets to Florida – from Maryland. We called and said it was a wonderful gift, but what about the itinerary? Christa and Steve said, "We decided we wanted to give you a trip, but we're giving it to you from Maryland, so you're going to have to come here and stay a while and visit with us. And when you come back from Florida, you'll again stay with us. That way we'll make sure you get a visit in." We went down before the trip and stayed with them for a few days and had a wonderful time – then on to Florida. After visiting friends in Miami, we rented a car, headed up to Fort Lauderdale, and then drove on to Palm Beach, where my uncle had a home. We went on to Orlando for a few days, and then went back to Maryland. When we got to Maryland, we enjoyed telling Christa and Steve about our adventures. They had tickets for the Kennedy Center to hear Tony Bennett. The four of us took off for an evening of dinner and a show.

While we were in Disney World, we bought a pair of gilt ceramic doves, with the male's wings spread out protecting the female. I didn't want to check them because they were rather fragile, so I had them put in a large box with a lot of protective wrapping. We carried the box on the plane when we left Florida. The stewardess said, "Where are you bound for? I hope this will be your last flight, because this box really will have to go into a storage compartment." So when we said we were stopping over in Maryland and then going on to Boston, she said, "When you make arrangements for the next flight, make sure the plane has a large enough compartment for the package, otherwise you may have a problem getting on the plane with a box this large." Then she took our package off to be stored. Once the flight was ended, she gave it back to us. When we were ready to leave Maryland, I called the airline to confirm our reservations. Reaching the reservation clerk, I said, "I have a very large package with me and I was told there had to be enough room on the plane. Is this a large plane?"

The fellow on the end of line said, "Well, lady, I don't know what you mean by a large plane."

"I have this big package," I replied, "and I need enough room for it to be put in a compartment."

As I was talking to the baffled clerk, I looked up, and there were Christa, Steve, and Ed all shaking with laughter. When I hung up, they said, "We could almost see the man on the other end of the phone saying, "But, lady, they're *all* large planes!"

Our twenty-fifth wedding anniversary was on July 26, 1972. The previous Thanksgiving, Christa and Steve were home from Maryland, and Stephen and Kit were home from college. Together they made arrangements for an anniversary celebration and for a gift of their portrait. Without our knowledge, they had a sitting during the Christmas holidays. Christa said afterward that trying to get everyone together, dressed for a picture, and out of the house without it looking suspicious to Ed and me was really a challenge. At Easter, they were again all at home together and were able to look at the proofs to make a choice.

From her home in Maryland, Christa planned the party, delegating certain jobs for each brother or sister, sending out the invitations, and keeping in touch with Lisa and Betsy to make sure they kept us from knowing what was going on. They pulled it off. That Saturday at two o'clock, relatives, friends, and neighbors appeared along with flowers, decorations, food, and drink. Ed and I were not only surprised, but very touched. We hung the picture over the fireplace in the living room.

Some time later, Ed and I planned a trip to California, driving up the coast from Los Angeles to San Francisco, visiting friends, and then going off to Hawaii. On our return, we were going to Caesar's Palace in Las Vegas. Christa and Steve came down from New Hampshire to say good-bye and take us to the airport. Christa had made me a wardrobe: a seersucker sundress, a printed dress with a jacket, a traveling suit of four pieces – skirt, jacket, slacks, and lined vest – all coordinated. Christa and Steve also gave us an envelope with $200 in it. They said, "This is just plain extra, so when you get to Las Vegas you can have fun playing the slot machines."

Family Pets

When Christa was preparing to leave for Maryland after the wedding, our black cat had a litter of kittens. Christa had hoped to take two of them with her, but she and Steve were told that pets were not allowed in the apartment complex. However, after they had been there awhile, she wrote, "I'm so mad not to have taken the kittens. There are animals all over the place! Dogs, cats, what have you! I keep looking for a 'free kitten' sign, but so far, no luck. I think the only catch is if the office finds out you have an animal, they might charge you for it. But since we are in the farthest corner of the project, I don't think they'd know."

An acquaintance of mine had kittens that she was giving away. The next time Christa and Steve visited, they chose two of them: a gray one they named Rizzo and a black one, Bear Cat. Christa later wrote:

We had a fire upstairs in the building – nothing serious, just a grease fire in the kitchen, but I was in the bedroom sewing and didn't hear the fire engine that *parked* on the front lawn. I didn't smell the smoke, but heard the kittens crying. When I looked out the front window and saw firemen running into the building with hoses, I grabbed the cats and ran. The whole thing lasted two minutes. I think the woman upstairs had the fire out by the time the truck arrived. What bothered me was that no one knocked on the door to let me know!

We've been letting the cats out by themselves. Rizzo got confused and went up to the third floor and cried to come in. Bear goes out and rolls around in the dirt and then wants to come in. He also caught and killed a bird last week. He's so darn quick. Steve let him have the bird and so far he's behaving.

We have collars on the cats, and since they have grown quite a bit, I was afraid Bear's was a little tight. So, last week Steve took it off and put it on the deacon's bench. The cat kept nudging it – he wanted it back on! Steve made another hole in the collar and put it back on, and Bear was content. And you should have seen them trying to get those things off when we first put the collars on!

One day Bear Cat did not come home. They looked all over the neighborhood for him. They knocked on doors and asked everyone they saw. They put notices up in the office and surrounding stores. No black cat. Even after a couple of months, they would expect him at the door. Finally they accepted the fact that he was gone.

Rizzo had kittens. They made a comfortable spot for her in the back room, a combination study, guest room, and storage area. There the kittens could be nice and quiet. When they began to get a little bigger, Christa wrote, "Our bedroom is a menagerie. Rizzo does not like to have the kittens in the back room. They crawl over the barricade I made. So where do they sleep? On the bed, of course! Rizzo yells at me every time I go by. She's waiting for me to yank them off. That does no good because they are back up there in two minutes . . . Last night we got ready to go to sleep and found a *wet* sheet! Unfortunately, the kittens are not completely trained, but they do make it to the kitty litter most of the time."

From Rizzo's first litter of kittens, Christa and Steve kept a little black female and called her Jo Cat. When Rizzo had her second litter, they kept a chubby male named Willie. Then they had their cat family neutered. Willie loved the outdoors and would stay out for hours. Jo would go out, but she would come back in to use the kitty litter. When they moved to New Hampshire, they had an opening cut into the outside door leading down to the basement. The cats could then come and go as they pleased, and they had a cozy place of their own. Jo and Willie thought that was fine, but Rizzo preferred the house. She had to be with her people. She demanded and received a lot of attention and would spend hours in Christa's arms if Christa would let her. After each child was born, Rizzo was attentive to them. If one of them were not feeling well, she would stay by the child's side and worry over it.

Occasionally we took our dog, Jessie, with us when we visited. Rizzo would show her displeasure and leave. There were times when Christa would dog-sit for us, and Jessie would be there for a few days. On one occasion, Jessie was with them for quite a long time – the poor cat was a wreck! Christa tried to get Rizzo to stay in the house and become friends with Jessie, but the cat would have none of that. After we took Jessie home, Rizzo took over the house, examined every corner, and then demanded complete attention for days.

When Christa was selected for the space shuttle, the cats were getting old, although they were still frisky and healthy. The children wanted a dog, and Christa wanted them to have one, but only after her year's commitment to NASA was over. She didn't feel that it would be fair for Steve to have to handle the kids, the house, and also house-break a dog.

Hansi and Bill Glahn, friends of Christa and Steve's, have a springer spaniel named Patrick. Scott and Ben Glahn are best friends, so when Patrick became the father of a litter in the summer of 1986, the Glahns gave Scott and Caroline their choice of the new puppies. The children went to visit the pups often and tried to decide which one they wanted for their own. We went with them a couple of times. The pups were so cute that it was difficult to decide. Caroline and Scott finally chose a brown and white pup that they named Charlie.

Rizzo tolerated the dog as she came to realize that she had to share the house with him. He chased the cats around, but it was only in fun. Advanced in years, Rizzo died peacefully the next Christmas season.

Uncle Philip

Christa wrote on January 3, 1971, after she and Steve arrived home in District Heights, Maryland, from their Christmas visit to us, "As usual, we forgot a few things – Steve's shoes, my brown shoes, my new guitar book. We were literally snowed in New Jersey on New Year's Day, but we did manage to see Uncle Philip and Aunt Mary. (By the way, I left my boots at their house!) They took us out to lunch and showed us Princeton.

"Uncle Philip gave me a copy of one of his lectures, and they gave us a letter opener. We are sending them a print – what else!? – and a note of thanks." (The National Gallery of Art was a favorite place of Christa's, and we were all recipients of prints she chose from the gift shop.) "I really enjoyed myself, and Uncle Philip and Steve got along fine. I showed them our wedding pictures."

Aunt Mary had written on October 11, 1970, that they found Christa's wedding announcement when they returned from a trip abroad. Uncle Philip was a trustee of the American University in Beirut, Lebanon. Every summer, he attended the annual trustee meeting, and then he and Aunt Mary would stay abroad for three or four months, the two of them traveling as Uncle Philip gave lectures. After Christa and Steve's first visit, Aunt Mary wrote how much she enjoyed seeing Christa again and that they were pleased to meet Steve. She hoped Christa and Steve would stop to see them often.

When Uncle Philip wrote in 1975 that Aunt Mary was in the hospital, he also sent me congratulations about going back to school. "It is never too late to learn. It is, of course, not the diploma that counts, but the learning that widens your horizons, deepens your sympathies, makes you a more useful mother, wife, and member of the community, and makes your life richer and larger."

By January 1977, Aunt Mary had died and Uncle Philip was alone. Christa, Steve, and four-month-old Scott stopped in Princeton on their way back home from spending the holidays with us. Christa was touched by the way Uncle Philip took to the baby. She put Scott on his lap, and when the baby smiled, Uncle Philip became excited. "He knows me, Christa! He knows his Uncle Philip!"

Christa called me one day in tears – she had just read of Uncle

Philip's death in *Time* magazine. He had died December 24, 1978, but we learned of it only through Christa's reading the notice in the magazine.

Aunt Carrie

Late in 1973, Christa and Steve decided to spend a weekend in New York with Aunt Carrie and see the Metropolitan Opera production of *Faust*. They drove up to New Jersey, left their car with Jack and Judy Sheedy (Jack was a classmate of Steve's from VMI), and took the tube into the city.

They thoroughly enjoyed the opera and then dinner at Luchow's with Aunt Carrie, but were distressed because Aunt Carrie's sight had failed to the extent that they felt she should not be living alone. After discussing the situation, they decided to ask her to come to live with them. As their apartment was on the ground floor, she wouldn't have any stairs to climb, and they had a large extra room that they could move into for their bedroom. Aunt Carrie could then have their room. They asked what we thought.

It seemed to us to be quite an undertaking, but Ed felt that because they were so many generations apart, they would probably get along just fine. But Aunt Carrie had always lived alone and had always lived in New York City. Would she agree to move to the Washington area and could she be happy there? We commended them for their kindness and said that we would do what we could to help. So they called her and extended the invitation. She said, "Oh my goodness, how wonderful of you, but no, I'd just be in your way."

Aunt Carrie and Ed's family spent Christmas of 1973 with us in Framingham. On January 29, 1974, Aunt Carrie would be 89 years old. We decided, since we were all together at Christmas, that we would surprise her with an early birthday party. Birthdays were always elaborate occasions in our family, so we didn't anticipate the delight and amazement that the party would be for Aunt Carrie. She had never had a party before with a home-baked birthday cake and candles.

At first, Christa and Steve tried to make living with them sound exciting. They told her about the great museums, theaters, concerts, and symphonies in their area. And if she wanted, she could join a golden age group. Aunt Carrie answered that most activities were beyond her capabilities, so Christa and Steve changed their tactics by saying that they had only suggested them because they didn't want her to think that she had to sit around all day if she didn't want to. Whatever she wanted to do – or not do – would be fine.

They finally convinced her that they really wanted her and that the move would be good for all of them. Since it was Steve who had originally suggested the idea, Aunt Carrie felt that Christa wasn't foisting her relatives on him.

Later Christa and Sue Rowold drove up to Framingham. The next day, the three of us went to New York to help Aunt Carrie pack and close up her apartment. We found her trying to get rid of her things by giving or throwing them away. We tried to convince her to keep whatever she wanted. This was to be her home. She had already given away her piano, which was a shame since she still enjoyed playing. Luckily, I was able to rescue some old snapshots and photographs. She thought that no one would want those old things! I hate to imagine what had already found its way to the trash. We saved a beautifully carved pentagon-shaped table and two upholstered chairs with carved wood trim and claw feet.

Steve and Carl Rowold, Sue's husband, met us in New York. They packed a rented U-Haul truck and the cars, and then we took off for Maryland. Aunt Carrie, with never a backward glance or a reference that she was leaving a city that had been her home for almost ninety years, was looking forward to her new home and not being alone.

Soon thereafter, Christa called us with the news that they just bought a house. She was laughing because they really had not been intending to buy a house, but this one just happened to be on the market and the circumstances were right. "We will have so much more room, and Aunt Carrie's bedroom will be larger. She should enjoy walking around her own yard and sitting in the sun."

The McAuliffe house was a split-level with three bedrooms in Oxon Hill, Maryland. It had a lovely yard surrounded by a split-rail fence. Aunt Carrie adapted easily to her new environment. She and Steve spent many an hour in friendly argument over the relative merits of the Irish and the Germans. She delighted Christa, Steve, and their friends with stories of old New York, Tammany Hall, and Al Smith. She told of the family's friendship with Archbishop Rummel of New Orleans and of her southern friends. She described her trips abroad by ship, some with dignitaries of the Church, and of her meetings with Popes Pius XI and

Pius XII. She had worked considerably beyond the age of retirement, managing an insurance office, and spoke with affection of her "girls." In the 1930s she fought and won a battle to hire a blind typist and have her seeing-eye dog in the office. She proved to be one of her best workers. I remember going to the office as a little girl and being allowed to speak to the dog, but not to touch.

Many a time when Christa and Steve had a party, some of their guests would find their way to Aunt Carrie's room to say hello and then stay to talk. They would ask her about life at the turn of the century, politics, and prohibition.

On Halloween of 1974, Christa and Steve planned a party for about forty guests. Just before the party, Christa remarked, "I sure hope everyone wears a costume this year. Last year we had a few show up without one."

Later, after everyone had arrived and the party was in full swing on the lower level, the doorbell rang. Aunt Carrie called to Christa, but when she didn't get an answer, she trotted down the hallway and opened the door herself. In the doorway stood a large figure in a flowing black cloak, his face painted white and fangs protruding over his lower lip. Aunt Carrie peered out at him in the darkness and said, "Well, I guess you can join the party, but Christa is going to be upset. You were supposed to come in costume!"

Sue and Carl Rowold and their baby were often at the house. Aunt Carrie made a great fuss over Matthew. She would coo to him, cradle him, and bounce him gently. Usually Matt would cry and fuss. Sue and Christa would cringe and try to get the baby to be content with Aunt Carrie's attention, but it didn't seem to bother her – she always looked forward to their coming and thought Matthew was something special. It was the first occasion that she had had to be around a baby for any length of time.

Christa wrote that February: "We got a note from one of Aunt Carrie's friend's daughters saying that her mother had died last week. Apparently, Jo Schlomer was Aunt Carrie's oldest friend – she would have been 90 in August. Last fall, Jo fell and broke her pelvis. She was placed in a nursing home. I feel so bad for Aunt Carrie, but she always takes everything right in stride."

On March 12 she wrote: "Aunt Carrie is doing fine. We did forget to bring some beer up from downstairs for her on Monday. Both of us had classes that night, and she knew we wouldn't be home until late, so she decided to brave the trip downstairs herself. Everything went fine until Aunt Carrie – six-pack in hand – tried to open the door. There sat Willie-cat blocking her way. After a few minutes (of course, Willie never moved), she decided to open the closet door. Sure enough, he scooted right in there. So Aunt Carrie came upstairs, put the beer in the refrigerator, and went down to release the captive. This escapade must have taken an hour at least! I wish I had seen it!"

On Saturday, May 31, Ed's mother, his brother Jim, and Helen stopped at Christa's on their way home from Florida. Aunt Carrie and Mom always got along well and enjoyed each other's company. After a pleasant visit and dinner, they left in the early evening for Connecticut.

The next day, Sunday, June 1, 1975, Christa, Steve, and Aunt Carrie planned on going to eleven o'clock Mass. Aunt Carrie was dressed and ready. She said she felt a little tired, and since there was time, she would go to her room and rest. Fifteen minutes later, Christa went to call her. When she didn't answer, Christa went into her room and found her lying on her bed. She had died. Christa called us in tears, and we immediately made arrangements to be on the next available flight to Maryland. We notified relatives. Poor Mom   she just couldn't believe it and kept saying, "But we were just with her yesterday!"

Steve had Aunt Carrie's will and knew that her jewelry and whatever was left of her estate after funeral expenses would go to the Church to educate young men for the priesthood. She had written me in 1969 that her affairs were all in order in the event of her death and that any assistance I could give the executor would be appreciated. I agreed, and the subject was not brought up again. But we found that we did have a problem. We didn't know where she was to be buried. We called the executor in New York, and she had no idea. We called those with whom she had kept in touch, but no one could help us. Finally we located the cemetery in Brooklyn where her mother and father were buried. But we could find nothing to prove she had a right to be buried there. There was, however, one unused grave left in the family plot. We left it up to the funeral home and cemetery to make the necessary arrangements. There was another problem. The graves in the very old cemetery were too narrow for a regular casket. We had to order a special casket in New York. Aunt Carrie's body would be sent to New York by train, there the casket would be changed, and then her casket would be taken to a chapel in Brooklyn where we would have the services.

We drove to New Jersey, stayed with Jack and Judy Sheedy overnight, and left early for the funeral. During the graveside services, we were plagued by the thought that someone might ask us for proof that this grave belonged to her. Then what would happen? Fortunately, Aunt Carrie's right to be buried there was not challenged.

Aunt Carrie enjoyed her last year of life living with Christa and Steve. They provided her with a happy, comfortable home, and she enriched their lives.

Christa's Family Grows (and Moves)

On Sunday, September 11, 1976, Scott Corrigan McAuliffe made his appearance at 5:00 a.m. in the hospital at Andrews Air Force Base. Ed and I arrived late that afternoon to find a beaming Steve and a radiant Christa. One of her first comments was "How appropriate for a social studies teacher to have a Bicentennial baby!"

Later that fall, Christa, Steve, and Scott drove up from Maryland. Ed and I were delighted that they were having the baby baptized at St. Jeremiah's, and Ed was particularly pleased to have his first grandchild wear the christening dress that his grandmother made for him in 1922.

We gathered at our house for a celebration after the church service. Steve had taken slides of Christa during all the stages of her pregnancy, including the baby's birth. During the party he set up the screen and slide projector in one bedroom and ran the slides with a commentary a couple of times for those interested in seeing them. One of the viewers was Christa's young cousin Marion, who remarked as she left the room, "I can't wait to get married and have a baby of my own!"

Christa and Steve went to visit their friends Polly and Terry Shumaker, who had moved to New Hampshire. Christa was taken with the state and the way of life that the Shumakers had there. When it was time for Steve to leave the army, he considered taking a position in Congressman Hoyer's law firm in Washington. But six years in that area was enough for Christa. "I don't want to raise a family here. I want the peace and quiet of New Hampshire." So Steve applied to the attorney general's office in Concord, and when he was accepted, they put their Maryland home on the market.

Scott was only a baby when Christa and Steve moved to a Victorian house in Concord, New Hampshire. The McAuliffe family sent out cards announcing that they had "moved to the snowy northeast. Come up to see us soon and bring sweaters!" They tackled the job of making the wonderful old Victorian house livable, of coping with a new baby, of taking new jobs, and of making new friends. The first year Christa taught part-time at Rundlett Junior High School in Concord.

The Jordans moved to Concord a year later, also coming up from Washington, D.C., so David could take a job with the state attorney general's office. Christa and Jo Ann went to the annual New Hampshire Bar Association meeting together. They knew none of the other women; as they watched all the sophisticated spouses, they wondered if they would ever be like them when they got older.

Christa and Jo Ann formed a preschool group with Hansi Glahn, Eileen Gfroerer, and Jane Funk. Every Wednesday afternoon, they took turns watching each other's children for two hours, so the others would have some free time. They looked forward to those free Wednesday afternoons. No matter what the weather was like – rain, snow, or sun – the kids would be brought to the home of the woman whose turn it was to watch them, so their mothers could have two hours to do whatever needed to be done without children. Since all the children were being toilet-trained, whoever had them would pray that they would get through the two hours without any accidents.

The women also formed a food co-op. They thought they would save money by buying food in bulk. Once a month they climbed into Jane's truck and headed for a Manchester wholesaler. They would go into a warehouse and pretend that they were buying for a grocery store. They'd come back with hundred-pound bags of flour and sugar, cereal by the case, sacks of bulgur wheat, and gallons of pickles. In the cold of winter, they would divide the huge sacks of food in Jo Ann's barn. Christa used to bring me spices, peanut butter, and whatever else they were sharing. They laughed about getting it and dividing it up, but their families didn't think it so funny. The kids used to complain to one another about having the same kind of cereal to eat for a month. Jo Ann said that she finally got rid of everything last year, except for a gallon jar full of baking cocoa!

Caroline's Birth

Christa's second baby was due in the middle of August 1979. When she asked me to be present at the birth, I was pleased not only because Christa wanted me there, but also because none of my children had been born naturally, without anesthesia, and I felt that something was missing in my experiences. While I was having my family, natural childbirth was not common. I did discuss going through natural childbirth with my doctor when I carried my fourth child, Lisa. My doctor gave me a set of exercises to do and no encouragement. At the delivery, he was out of the country. It was not a successful natural childbirth.

Second births sometimes come earlier, so to be on the safe side, I went to Concord two weeks before the due date. We spent the days leisurely readying the baby's room, rearranging pantry shelves, shopping, and taking Scott swimming and on picnics. Ed came up to spend the weekends with us.

Christa's due date came and passed by. I had commitments on the calendar that I canceled. Steve teased, "The minute you leave town, we'll probably head to the hospital." But I was determined that I was going to be there when this baby came into the world.

We went to the midwife once a week, and then twice a week. Everything was fine, the baby's heartbeat was strong, and we were told it sounded like a boy's.

Two weeks overdue! Steve took us out to dinner on August 23, their seventh anniversary. A restaurant in the old Concord jail specialized in margueritas and prime rib – we had both.

Finally it was time – early the next morning, after the sitter arrived, we left for the hospital. Included with Christa's overnight bag was a party basket for all of us – to celebrate.

The delivery room was a private room with bright flowered curtains on the windows. This was a far cry from the white sterile rooms I had shared with others.

The baby's heart was monitored continuously. "It still sounds like a boy," we were told. Steve and Christa worked together, he rubbing her back and coaching her breathing. The midwife was encouraging and calm. When the baby's head started to appear and the birth didn't follow right away, I moved away from the bed and began pacing up and down by the windows, not wanting to interrupt their concentration. But Christa laughed at me, "What's the matter, Mom? Nervous?" Yes . . .

Caroline, named after Aunt Carrie, was eased into the world. Christa and I both yelped. We had our girl! Steve was beaming; hugs and kisses and a tear or two followed. Three generations of women – we had our girl!

The nurse wheeled in the bathing supplies, and I had the honor of giving Caroline her first bath. Dressed in a shirt and diaper and wrapped in a soft receiving blanket, the clean little one was put into her crib. Christa called her father and Steve's mother and dad to tell them about their new granddaughter.

From the party basket we toasted the birth and the health of mother and child. Then we left the delivery room, Christa wheeling the crib before her. When she and the baby were settled, we left her to get a little rest. Steve went to the office to spread the news, and I went home to Scott.

After Scott had his breakfast and was dressed, we went back to the hospital. We put on green hospital gowns and met Christa and Caroline in the visiting room. Scott hugged his mother and then tentatively played with Caroline's fingers, saying, "She's so tiny."

Ed arrived bringing flowers for his girls. He loved babies, and little girls melted his heart. Caroline was his joy; as she grew, she delighted him. "She's going to be a classic beauty," he would say.

Christa came home from the hospital the next day. Then, I had to go home. Christa felt fine, and I was assured that they would manage. They had plenty of friends and plenty of help. And I had been gone from my home a month. It was a great experience to be with them, and now we had two grandchildren to love. Yet I still felt miserable leaving them.

Teaching in New Hampshire

Shortly after Caroline's birth, Christa had an opportunity for a position at Bow Memorial School, teaching social studies in the seventh and eighth grades, and later teaching English in the ninth grade. Christa found a sitter near school so she could drop Caroline off in the mornings and go over to feed her during breaks in classes. That arrangement worked out fine.

One of Christa's friends, Eileen O'Hara, lived with Christa and Steve while she looked for an apartment. Eileen, Christa, and Carol Bradley taught together and shared open classrooms; only panels of orange, yellow, and beige partially separated their teaching areas. Christa had covered her large wall with a collage of *Time* magazine covers which she used as a source of discussion for writing exercises and current events.

Christa taught English lessons to the ninth-grade students by using the driver's handbook. "These kids are nearing driving age. This connects them with the real world." Following the manual, the students debated by taking the viewpoints of a police officer and a driver, wrote stories and essays, and learned the rules of the road for the state of New Hampshire.

One day, Scott did not have a sitter, so Christa chose to bring him to school with her rather than stay at home with him. She, Carol, and Eileen spent the day shuffling him between them so no one would know that he was at school – except, of course, for the students in their classes who got a big charge out of having a three-year-old classmate.

Christa started a Faculty Advisory Committee at Bow Memorial School based on one that was used at Thomas Johnson in Maryland. One representative from each grade met together once a week, and they established their own agenda forum for teachers. They would troubleshoot and act as a voice for the teachers to the principal.

After a few years in New Hampshire, Christa decided that she needed experience teaching at the high school level, so she found a job at Concord High for the 1982–83 school year. As she wrote her sister Betsy, "I'm looking forward to my debut as a high school teacher. It should be fun. It will also keep me busy with new material this year; I want to make sure I'm challenging the students enough." She also noted with parental surprise, "Scott will be six soon and starting kindergarten. That doesn't seem possible. He's so grown up!"

Carol

Christa convinced her friend and fellow teacher Carol Bradley to go for her master's degree. Christa intended to become a principal, and she wanted Carol to be her assistant principal. She also convinced the Bradleys to move into Concord so they would be closer to her. That way, when she and Carol became principal and assistant principal, they could ride or walk to school together.

The Bradleys found and bought a house a short distance from Christa and Steve's. The house needed extensive repair work, which took a long time, but they were able to move in (with no hookups and no TV) after Christa had left for Houston.

Carol was disappointed not to have Christa around when they moved in. She and Christa had shared so much in having the house done over, and Carol felt that it would be a long time before Christa could see the results. Carol was surprised to look out the window one day to see Christa, on her first visit home from Houston, standing in the driveway.

"Well, do I get to see my house?" Christa asked.

"Quick! I'll give you a tour before you have to take off again!"

That weekend Christa was to be interviewed on WKXL, a local radio station. Just as she was leaving for the interview, she found that her car wouldn't start. She called Carol and asked her to come quickly so she wouldn't be late. Carol jumped into her car, still in her nightgown, and picked Christa up. As Christa got out of the car and ran into the station, she called over her shoulder, "I don't know how long this will last. Will you get out and ask someone so you can take me home?"

"But I'm in my nightgown!" Carol called out, but Christa was already gone. "Oh well," Carol shrugged, and then went in to check.

Carol did earn her master's degree and is now vice principal at John Stark Regional High School. Carol was among forty candidates to be interviewed for the position in May of 1987. She was given the job not only because she had the credentials but because she also had the same philosophy and the same spirit as Christa.

Innovations in the Classroom

Christa taught three law classes after she joined the Concord High School faculty, and involved her students directly with the court system. She did get a certain amount of good-humored teasing from other teachers because she would take her students out on field trips that sometimes ran longer than anticipated. When this happened, the students would return late for their next class; Christa found herself dubbed "Queen of the Field Trips."

The New Hampshire Bar Association matched a volunteer attorney with an appropriate classroom so the teacher would have a source of information about the legal system. On New Hampshire Law Day, the schoolchildren would participate as a training videotape was made of the attorneys as they conducted a mock trial. The "case" would be tried in the Concord District Court; next the students and participants would travel by bus to the Merrimack Superior Court, and then on to the New Hampshire Supreme Court, where the "case" would be tried for the final time. "Teaching the law," Christa believed, "is not just facts. Its value is in its vision of who we were and are, and who we want to be."

In addition to her interest in the legal system, Christa developed classes on the role and history of women in the United States. At first, she encountered trouble in getting her women's course accepted at her school, but she kept pushing until it was. In April of 1984, she wrote, "My Women's Class is doing well – I think I'll probably have one section of that next year." One of Christa's students wrote, "Mrs. McAuliffe's course on the American woman changed my outlook on life. It was like she discovered something new every day, and she was so excited about it that it got the rest of us excited, too."

Christa found that a good methodology was to include information from the direct experiences of seemingly ordinary women. Christa wrote, "In developing my course, *The American Woman,* I have discovered that much information about the social history of the United States has been found in diaries, travel accounts, and personal letters." Christa choose the film *Rosie the Riveter,* the story of a working woman during World War II, and set it up to play continuously on New Hampshire "Women in History Day" for anyone in the school to see. She wanted the students to realize how women came into the work force and to understand why many did not want to give up their jobs after the war.

Christa took a group of her students to Washington, D.C., to participate in "Close-Up," a full week of seminars, lectures, and tours of the important federal government buildings. Students from across the country were put into groups and had all their time planned – right down to recreation periods – by the leaders of the foundation sponsoring the event. The teachers accompanying the students were given the opportunity to attend lectures of their own.

One evening one of the boys that Christa had brought to Washington was missing. The foundation leaders were worried and sent out a missing persons bulletin. Christa was beside herself. This had never happened before. It was three o'clock in the morning, and all the adults were awake with worry, when the boy came sauntering back to his room. He had decided to explore Washington by himself without bothering to say anything to anyone. He even bragged about spending $100 for dinner.

"But why did you go away? Don't you know how dangerous it is for you to be by yourself in Washington?" Christa asked.

He answered, "What were you all worried about? It's my body. I can make my own decisions to go where I want to go."

Christa's reaction was, "If that is what you want to do, then you shouldn't get involved in a program like this!"

The same youngster signed up to go on another trip and was denied permission by the head of the department. The boy protested, and his mother claimed that he was being discriminated against. But he had proved that he couldn't be trusted, and neither he nor his family could understand that his own behavior had lost him his right to participate.

Christa was always a believer in the educational value of direct experience. And it did not have to be something as formal and complex as a field trip, much as she used them. During one of her lectures, Christa was speaking about food and mentioned ratatouille. "What's that?" asked one boy. Christa tried to explain and found it was just not in his realm of experience. The next day Christa came to school with a covered saucepan. At lunchtime she heated the contents and carried the pan into the cafeteria to the table where the young man was sitting with some of his friends. "Here you go. I brought you some ratatouille so you will know what it is." She put the pan down before him. He was embarrassed, but his friends were impressed; the boys ate every bit.

During the 1982–83 school year, Dudley Hughes came to Concord High as an exchange teacher from England. His wife, Pamela, and their children accompanied Dudley, and the Hughes and McAuliffe families became good friends. Zöe Hughes and Caroline were the same age, and the two Hughes boys were close to Scott's age.

One evening Steve and Christa, Dudley and Pamela Hughes, and Eileen O'Hara were standing in the doorway of the TV room talking while the five children were watching TV. Something rather stupid was going on, and Jonathan, the Hughes's oldest son remarked, "Well, that was a pretty Irish thing to do." The McAuliffes and Eileen O'Hara looked at one another. Dudley just grinned and shrugged.

The McAuliffes spent a month in England with the Hughes in the summer of 1984. Caroline and Zöe had missed each other, so Christa, Steve, and Scott left them to play together while they explored Shakespeare's birthplace, went to see *Richard III* at the Royal Shakespeare

Theater (which Scott loved), and took a rowboat ride on the Avon. Christa wrote that Scott was a wonderful companion, enjoying everything and eating everything. "I think he's on a growth spurt; the sleeves of the navy blazer you gave him for Christmas are starting to crawl up his arms."

Jo Ann

Christa had been running for some years, even competing in road races, such as the Bonne Bell ten kilometer race for women, and had become quite an advocate of the sport. She tried to convince her sisters Betsy and Lisa to enter the Bonne Bell with her; Lisa trained and got up to three miles a day, but tendonitis forced her to give up running. Christa's friend Jo Ann Jordan decided that she wanted to begin to run as well. After school, three days a week, the two would start off. Jo Ann's friendship with Christa proved more durable than her commitment to running. Later she reminisced:

When I decided I wanted to learn to jog, Christa offered to teach me. She ran routinely over the years. After school we would get our kids settled, usually watching TV, and off we would go. She had planned a two-mile route which we were to cover three days a week. We started out walking the route. We'd increase the pace, faster and faster, until we were running. I thought I was going to die. She didn't even breathe hard. She would chat away. I could barely breathe. She kept saying it would feel better soon. Our route was rather a "back roads" one until she was chosen to be the Teacher in Space. I believe it was unconscious, but we then began more main roads. People would wave and congratulate her while I was dying and gasping for air.

Christa was willing to try anything. We were working at a Spring Sports Sale sponsored by the Junior Service League and we saw a tent that slept six. It was on sale for $20. We got excited. What an experience this would be for the kids. We would pack them all in the car and go camping. We split the cost of the tent and hauled the musty, smelly tent home and set it up in my backyard. The kids ran in and out of it, and that was all the camping they ever did in it.

Many a hot summer day, before we had pool memberships, we would pack the kids into the car with food and drinks and spend the afternoon by Clough Pond. The kids would play in the sand and swim while we chatted on the beach.

Christa was very good at giving parties. She and Steve had an annual Halloween party. She would pack the house with people dressed in all kinds of costumes. One year no one seemed to be having Christmas parties. So at the last minute Christa said, why don't we have a dinner? Within a few days she set up a lovely dinner party with four other couples. We all got dressed up and had a special holiday dinner.

She was extremely thoughtful. She was always there when you needed her. She would always say yes. She'd send flowers for special events. When I got my Bachelor of Science degree, flowers arrived at my door with a big note of congratulation. During the winter of 1985, while I was teaching at Rundlett Junior High School, flowers were brought into my classroom one day. They were from Christa – just to thank me for helping her during the busy time when she was getting ready to go to Washington for the Teacher-in-Space finals.

After we bought our house we had a big living room with not much furniture and no rugs. I was having people over and Christa knew I felt like my living room was bare so she went up to her attic and brought over a lovely oriental rug for me to use until I got one.

While we both worked at Concord High School, we would have lunch together a lot. Many a lunch we would split a salad from the little store across the street from the school and just sit and talk. Christa was always there to encourage me and share her teaching experience with me. She taught me her system of grading and encouraged me to go for my Health Educator Certification. We shared our frustrations as mothers and teachers. I remember her completing her application for the Teacher-in-Space program. At first she never expected to be chosen, but loved the experience. It was fun to listen to her.

When she found out she was a finalist it was exciting. She was never one to be a fashion plate, so she needed a lot of new clothes, everything from underwear to dresses. A few times near the final week of school we would run out at lunch to pick out a few things. She wanted a nightgown that didn't look like a nightgown. Something she could answer the door in and it would be okay. She was so practical.

Our children attended Dewey School, and every Halloween they had a parade to celebrate. Christa always put me to shame. She would get patterns that her kids would choose, and they'd always have a beautiful hand-made costume. Mine would have store-bought of their choice. I'd marvel at how she would have the time and she'd say, "Oh, it doesn't take long." I don't know when she slept. She'd play tennis, volleyball, do her school work and still, when I'd call to suggest we do something, she always said yes.

After Caroline was born we decided to go out to dinner one evening to a

Mexican restaurant. Caroline was too young to leave at home. So the four of us went out. Caroline went along in a car bed and was placed under the table while we ate. No problem at all. Christa (and Caroline) were calm throughout the whole evening. We hardly knew she was there. Of course, Scott, Sandy, and David wondered why they could not go along too.

Christa's birthday was September 2 and mine is September 4. Every year at that time we would get together, have lunch or maybe just a drink and wish each other Happy Birthday and wonder what the year ahead would bring. It was always an exciting time. The kids would be starting school, having new teachers, ones that we agonized over requesting the previous June, hoping we were choosing the right ones and not traumatizing our children. We would be starting a new year at school, wondering what was in store for us.

The last time we were together we all went ice skating at Thayer Pond down the street. We played ice hockey with the kids, came back to my house, got out the paper plates, and had tuna-fish sandwiches. Certainly not a fancy meal, but we all had a good time.

I spoke with Christa the week before the shuttle was to go up. She was baking cookies for her new friends in the space program. I said to her that she would probably be so busy after the trip I would not see her for a while or – I joked – she'd be so famous I would never hear from her again. She said that was silly. She said, "I'll call you when I get back. That sounds funny. It sounds like I'm only going to New Jersey." I wished her luck. I told her I would be there watching.

Christa's Children

When Scott was five and Caroline two, Christa listed the children's characteristics and was amazed at how different their personalities were. In her notes, which were left in her school desk and found after the *Challenger* tragedy, Christa had jotted down the differences between her children:

It's a constant amazement to my husband and me that the same genetic structure could produce two such unique individuals. Scott, my delicate five-year-old, dark skinned Lebanese with those huge heavy-lidded eyes, and Caroline, my stocky, blue-eyed, ever-smiling Irish daughter . . . So sensitive is Scott that he turned off Sesame Street during an episode in which a cartoon mouse was eaten by a cartoon cat. His concern for others makes him a deviant of sibling rivalry – [he wants to] include his sister in everything – [he will say] she needs it too because she's our family. A perfectionist, he bursts into tears when letters he's been working on do not look right. He's an obedient love, aiming, hoping to please, and devastated with even the hint of disapproval. A quiet child whose happiest moments are watching the rain or snow fall, perched on his bed in a darkened room thinking his private thoughts.

Then there's Caroline, that burst of energy who flies everywhere to everywhere bubbling sometimes, "Hug, hug," and [sometimes] defiant . . . Miss Independence never has problems adjusting to sitters or a new situation, she greets the unknown like a lost friend – ready for anything. She lets you know what she wants when she wants it. She never asks for things – just demands. On Halloween night, by the second house she knew what to do. Bang on the door, hold open your bag, and move fast – on to the next treat. Her love of sweets and sugar equals her brother's disdain for the same. Leave her alone and take your chances – emptying the toilet with any kind of container makes wonderful fun; trashing rooms is her specialty. Isn't it strange how the paver of new ways came last?

They are so different, my children.

Christa taught Catholic Church Doctrine at St. Peter's Church in Concord. Scott was going for his first catechism lesson, so Christa walked him over to his class before going to hers. After class, Scott's teacher came up to Christa and reported, "I threw out a question in class: can anyone tell me where God lives? Scott raised his hand, so I called on him and he answered very seriously, 'Well, it's a little difficult to explain, but you see, God lives in another dimension . . .' Am I going to have trouble with this kid?"

The weekend of the announcement that Christa was to become the Teacher in Space was hectic in Concord, especially at the McAuliffe's. The phone and doorbell didn't stop ringing, and the police were trying to keep the newspeople under control. Everyone was trying to talk to Christa, and she was doing her best to keep up with appointments.

Lisa was helping out by getting Caroline ready for bed. She had her in the tub, Caroline complaining all the while that she wanted her mother to give her a bath. "Not tonight, Caroline, your mother is busy." An exasperated Caroline burst out, "I know, I know, I know! But I still want Mommy!"

Caroline was always sociable; anyone was a challenge to be won over as a friend. Once she was at the hairdresser with her mother as Christa was having her hair cut. Christa watched Caroline in the mirror as the little girl snuggled up to the right-hand side of her chair and looked up at the well-dressed woman sitting next to her reading a magazine. Christa waited to see what ploy Caroline would use this time to strike up a conversation. The five year old decided. "I love your pearls," Caroline said to the woman, "I would love some; tell me, where did you get them?"

Christa's farewell to her daughter was, "See ya later, alligator."

Block Island Visit

Betsy, our youngest daughter, graduated from North Adams College in the northwestern corner of Massachusetts in the spring of 1980. We drove up for the day in three cars. Ed, his mother, Kit, and I in the first car, Stephen, his future wife, Anne, and Lisa in the second, and Christa, Steve, and their two children in the third.

After the ceremonies, we went to Betsy's apartment and were able to pack up all her belongings in the three cars and take them home. One "belonging" was a four-month-old puppy named Jessie, a golden retriever and collie mix with a collie-shaped nose and white chest and paws. Never had I felt a puppy so soft.

Betsy acquired Jessie because she was living in an apartment that allowed dogs. Fellow classmates had brought the dog back to school after rescuing her from being tormented by kids on the Boston Common. They were unable to keep the dog in their dorm, so Jessie went to live with Betsy.

We were still upset over the death of our last dog, and Ed had said emphatically, "Enough! No more dogs!"

When he looked at the pup, Betsy said, "Don't worry, Dad, if I can't have her with me, I'll get one of my friends to take her."

That summer, Betsy got a job as a waitress on Block Island, Rhode Island. She was going to save money for a move to California. Jessie was left with us. "Don't worry, Dad. When I get home in the fall, my friend will take the dog."

Christa and I decided to visit Betsy for her twenty-second birthday on July 6, 1980. Betsy was delighted and reserved a room for us at Highview, the hotel where she worked. She sent us the ferry schedule and said she would meet each ferry from one o'clock on.

On a blistering hot day, we drove down to Point Judith, Rhode Island. With us were three-year-old Scott and eleven-month-old Caroline. We also had Jessie, baby gear, dog food and bowls, luggage, and birthday presents.

When we arrived at the pier, the twelve o'clock ferry was docked and being boarded. There was a long line at the ticket booth. I hopped out of the car with the dog to get our tickets while Christa parked the car. But it didn't do any good. The boat was filled. Since there are no advance sales, we had to wait in line until they started selling tickets for the next ferry. That meant a wait of over two hours in the hot sun. We decided that I would keep a place in line, and our luggage, piled at my side, would provide some shade for Jessie. Christa would walk down to the public beach with the children. Then, in about an hour, she would come back and relieve me, and I would take a walk with the children. Needless to say, by the time we were able to board, we were all wilted.

To board the ferry, we had to climb up open stairs. That was a job. The dog and baby had to be carried, and Scott had to be helped so that he wouldn't fall through the openings. All this, and trying to get our luggage up at the same time.

We finally settled ourselves on a long bench in the lounge. The ride was said to be fairly short, about forty-five minutes. Caroline was on Christa's lap, Scott sat between us, and Jessie was sitting at my feet. Everything was fine and it was a relief to be sitting together out of the hot sun. Soon the lounge became uncomfortably warm and the boat began to rock. The water was turbulent, and we really started to roll with the waves.

All of a sudden, Christa bolted for the outside railing and, holding on to Caroline, leaned over the rail to catch the wind. Scott began to complain, and I felt miserable. Thinking a ginger ale might soothe Scott's stomach, I gave him some money and watched as a passenger helped him purchase his drink. He was holding his cup carefully as he returned to the bench when the ferry gave a sudden lurch. Scott was thrown head-first into the side of a large metal trash barrel. I could hear the thud as his head hit. The cup of ginger ale flew into the air and landed on Jessie who immediately yelped and jumped onto the lap of the gentleman sitting across from us. Scott was screaming, and a good-size egg began to form on his forehead. I managed to retrieve some ice cubes from the lost drink to put on his head.

I tried to comfort him and calm him down. When he was just quietly sobbing, I was able to rescue Jessie from the passenger she had latched onto. Christa, hearing the commotion, looked over her shoulder through the doorway, saw that we were managing, and put her energies into hanging on to Caroline and herself. The trip seemed to last forever.

Thank goodness Betsy was there to greet us! We now had someone to help us. Our first question was, "How do we get off this island without going back on that ferry?" But after getting our bearings, we found Block Island delightful. Betsy worked only the dinner hour, so the rest of her time was free. We went swimming, hiking, biking, and exploring.

We bought a birthday cake and took it, along with our presents, to a little restaurant where we held Betsy's birthday party on the porch. A customer at the next table was quite taken with Caroline. He took a daisy from the vase on his table and offered it to her. Both of her hands were busy – one held a spoon and the other a piece of roll – but she wanted the flower. She solved her dilemma by reaching for and taking the daisy with her mouth! We all laughed at her with the daisy hanging out of her mouth. Christa took her picture and asked, "Now what are you going to do?"

Our alternative to the ferry was a light plane that carried six passengers a trip. With that as the only other option, we decided to give the ferry another chance. We prepared this time by taking Dramamine before leaving. The trip back was fine, as I guess it usually is. All things considered, we were glad we went to Block Island for Betsy's birthday.

That fall, Betsy came home and called the friend who was to take Jessie. Betsy reached her two days before this friend was to leave to spend a year in Spain. "Don't worry, Dad. I'll find someone before I leave for California." At that point, we really didn't want her to find anyone – Jessie was home.

Jessie is still with us. She was at the airport the evening of July 19, 1985, while we waited for Christa's plane to arrive after she had been selected for the NASA flight. Reporters writing about the crowd there mentioned that even Christa's dog was waiting.

Thanksgiving Weekend in Washington

In 1984 Christa and Eileen O'Hara went to the annual conference of the National Council for the Social Studies. Christa was a delegate from the New Hampshire Council for Social Studies, and Eileen represented social studies teachers in her school. While there they stayed with Pat Mangum. Each day Pat drove them down to the subway in the morning and picked them up in the evening.

At the conference, Christa had to sit in on the meetings because she was a delegate, but Eileen was free to check out everything else that was going on. As one of the meetings ended, Eileen grabbed Christa and ushered her into a room where the author Maya Angelou was speaking. "We can't miss this!" she said.

They also didn't miss picking up the Teacher-in-Space applications. These were on the display table in packets of glittering blue and silver. Looking through the application, they decided it looked worse than a term paper.

Running through National Airport to catch their flight home, they each carried four string bags jammed full of books and pamphlets. One of the bags exploded and sent the contents flying all over the place. Eileen became upset and then even more so because Christa thought the scene was wildly funny and started to laugh. Eileen then caught her spirit and joined in. "We made quite a picture, laughing like fools and trying to scoop up the literature and make room for it in already overstuffed bags."

At home, Steve read the Teacher-in-Space application and commented, "Go for it!"

Eileen was then working nights typing at Steve's law office. After Christa had finished writing out the application by hand, she went to the office. They typed the information into a computer and started to edit the material. (They nicknamed it "Pigs in Space.") When that was done, Eileen typed the application from the printout, staying late so Christa could get it into the mail by the February 1, 1985, deadline.

Girl Scout Troop 315

When Christa became a Brownie, I was the leader of her troop, staying with the girls one way or another until they finished Senior Scouting. To foster group spirit and pride, I expected them to be in full uniform when we attended church, or went on trips to museums or such places as the United Nations in New York. During junior high and high school, they did not like the attention given them when they were in uniform, and they were always finding some reason to avoid wearing their uniforms. Since it should be full uniform, the most frequently used excuse was that the hat was dirty, needed washing, and had not yet dried. Later, after they were grown and we would reminisce, they asked, "Mrs. C., didn't you wonder why you would sometimes be the only one to show up in uniform?"

The girls – now women – who made up my troop were of consistently high caliber. After we began to meet as adults, I marveled at their strengths. Not only were they wonderful mothers and accomplished career women, but they also were involved in their communities, politics, and the welfare of others.

On December 27, 1985, I acquired a keepsake that is very dear to me. I show this to anyone who comes into our home; a captive audience, no one escapes "Show and Tell." The "show" part is a framed 16 × 21-inch composite of twenty snapshots. The "tell" makes these pictures significant. The story really begins in 1978, the year that some members of my Senior Girl Scout troop had a reunion.

Christa was living in Concord then, and she called one Friday evening during the school Christmas vacation. "You will not believe who I have just been talking to!" Christa told me excitedly: "My phone rang, and when I picked it up, I heard a jumble of voices singing 'Girl Scouts Together,' with a lot of laughter thrown in. I finally sorted out what was going on. They are all at Joyce's home in Buxton, Maine. Carolyn was visiting Joyce, and Bonnie drove over from Vermont. Margie lives nearby in Portland, and joined them, too. Naturally, when they got together, they thought 'Girl Scouts' and of missing troop members. I called Anne, and she is driving up from Lowell in the morning to pick me up. Then we're off to Maine to join the others. Isn't that wonderful!"

"Great!" I said. "Bring back lots of news, and give them all my love."

Anne Donovan Malovich was entertaining dinner guests when she took Christa's call. She became very excited and tried to explain the circumstances to her friends. "No one seems to realize the importance of us all being together again," she commented. "The experiences we had shared in Scouting forged a bond that will always hold us together. We were still together at an age when most girls left Scouting. We all found even more in the program and each other as time went on."

At this get-together, they had such a good time that they planned the next one. It was to be in August 1979 when Carolyn Bain Bunick and Bonnie Bain Finnegan's mother, Jean Bain Sanborn, would be visiting from her home in Florida. Jean had been assistant leader to Troop 315, as had Joyce Eklund Knight's mother, Mary Eklund. We met at Carolyn's home in Danvers, Massachusetts, on a beautiful, sunny day. Many children were there, and it was great fun to get to know the children that we had not met before. Phil Bunick, Carolyn's husband, took over barbecuing and supervising games, leaving us to enjoy catching up on careers and families. We all agreed that the next meeting should be Columbus Day weekend at the Lodge in Camp Wabasso in Bradford, New Hampshire. The Lodge, where we used to camp, held many memories.

Christa had been involved in Girl Scouting since she was in the second grade. The troop fluctuated in size – girls coming and going – but a small core remained throughout. We used Camp Wabasso for both summer and winter camping. In the winter of 1964, some of the older girls had just turned sixteen and had their driver's licenses. They wanted a camping experience without adults, so they chose a winter weekend at Camp Wabasso's Lodge. With some trepidation, I sent their request in to the Girl Scout Council. It was granted.

I did have a stipulation. There was a caretaker on the premises, but it was still a rather deserted area in winter, so I wanted them to take along our boxer dog, Sugar, for added protection.

They went off in three cars – girls, skis, and dog. The trip from Framingham takes about two hours. On Route 93, they pulled over to offer assistance to a stranded motorist; she had been there for hours, and they were the first to stop. Later the grateful motorist took the time to call me to say that the Girl Scouts had done their good deed for that day.

Sunday night they arrived back home, proud of themselves and excited about their weekend. There was only one flaw, and that was Sugar. She was homesick, kept whining, wouldn't climb the stairs, and finally threw up. "So next time, *please* can we leave her at home?"

I had fewer concerns when the girls, now wives and mothers, went back for that Columbus Day weekend in 1979. Plans were made and permission was again given for us to camp at the Lodge. Anne and Christa were the first to arrive that Friday. The key that they had would not fit into the lock, and the sign over the door now read "Infirmary." It was unthinkable to stay anywhere but in their Lodge, so they looked for a way to get in. A window in the kitchen was unlatched and they were able to get it open. All they had to do now was get in! Anne was seven months pregnant, and it was difficult for her to boost Christa up, so Christa boosted Anne through the window. They were glad no one was around to see that. They were cozily settled by the time the rest of us arrived.

Later, the caretaker came by to check and was perplexed. "I thought you were to be staying at the Lodge."

"Oh no," everyone assured him, "this is where we always stay." When we made arrangements with the council, we didn't know that they had changed what we knew as the "Lodge" to the camp's "Infirmary" and had built a new "Lodge."

This "Infirmary" became our retreat house twice each year, spring and fall. It was a place for renewal of spirit and friendship, lively conversations, quiet times, spontaneous laughter, long walks through the woods, and reading the Sunday paper while drifting in canoes on Lake Blaisdell. We played games, sang, and had popcorn and wine before a blazing fire.

I was very proud of them all; I never heard an unkind word spoken. I marveled at their ease and companionship with each other. They were caring, good, moral, and strong women, with families, careers, and a social consciousness that led them to contribute to the betterment of society. They all loved life. They really hadn't changed; they had only grown from young exciting girls into mature exciting women.

They enjoyed ribbing me, but they never forgot that I had been their leader. They never felt able to call me by my first name. Yet we were comfortable with each other. I could still refer to them as "girls," but they wouldn't let anyone else get away with that.

In October 1985, Christa came home from Houston for a few days and spent part of that time at Camp Wabasso with the troop. I wasn't able to be with them. They were all so excited about Christa's celebrity. Bonnie brought champagne to toast her, but Christa would have none of that: the toast was going to be "to all of us, as it always has been and always will be." They planned a third 1985 reunion that weekend. Since I was missing at the October session, it would have to be made up: I wasn't going to be allowed to get off that easily!

Two days after Christmas of 1985, Ed suggested that we go out to dinner. He said it was a surprise and that we were going to a place where we hadn't been for a long time. After driving for a half hour in softly falling snow, we came to the Rusty Scupper restaurant in Acton, Massachusetts. Ed spoke to the hostess, and she led us up the stairs to a corner area that seemed to be filled. "I think she's making a mistake," I whispered to Ed, and I was really bewildered when he just kept urging me forward.

It was then that I recognized Jean and Mary in the dim light. They were laughing. Jean lives in Florida, and Mary in Maine – what on earth was going on? Then I looked around the table, and there was Joyce, who also lives in Maine, and Bonnie from Vermont. Carolyn was up from Connecticut; Margie and Anne from Franklin and Lowell, Massachusetts; and Christa was there as well. But Christa and her family had just left our home the day before after spending the holidays with us! They were all grinning like Cheshire cats for putting one over on me. Ed started to leave, but they persuaded him to join us. What fun – such an unexpected, pleasurable evening. Later Anne said, "You know, it was great that Mr. C. wanted to stay and was comfortable with us."

When they were at the salad bar, Joyce could no longer contain the fact that they were there with the Teacher in Space. A busboy replenishing the salad bar became her victim. "Do you know we have a celebrity with us?" she asked him as Christa dug her elbow into Joyce's ribs – but Joyce went on and made the poor kid look at Christa until he admitted, whether he knew her or not, that of course he knew that she was the Teacher in Space. They came back to the table laughing, and Joyce maintained that she wanted everyone in the restaurant to be aware that Christa was the one who was going to fly the next month.

And I was given a present. It was a framed composite with pictures not only of the camp, lake, canoeing, and all of us, but also of all the girls and their families. There was one of Joyce's three boys, Jamie, Joshua, and Jeremy; a picture of Carolyn with her girls, Carrie, Sarah, and Jenny; one of Margie holding baby Laurie with her son Dan standing alongside. Bonnie's Kate and Keelan were together, and Anne's Erica, dressed in her Brownie uniform and sash, was standing by a fireplace next to her grinning brother Danny. Christa's Scott had a football in his hand, ready to throw it, and Caroline was all decked out in her hockey outfit. Even our dog, Jessie, made the picture.

It was still snowing at midnight when we left the restaurant. We grouped in the parking lot while saying good-bye, and Christa handed out Teacher-in-Space posters and patches that she brought along for classrooms and for their children. Everyone was hugged and kissed.

"Good-bye!"

"Drive carefully."

"See you in Florida."

"Have a great launch."

It was a wonderful evening; I think of December 27, 1985, each time I look at that composite photograph, my special keepsake of that evening.

On January 28, 1987, five "girls" from our troop arrived to spend the day with Ed and me, some traveling as long as three hours each way. With the Marascos from Lenox and the Wohlers, we all attended Mass at St. Jeremiah's Church in the morning and a service at Marian High School that evening.

One Saturday not too long ago, Lisa, her husband, Bob, and their baby, Michael, were visiting. Around noon, I looked out the window to see who was pulling into the driveway and saw Anne. Then I saw another car with Carolyn, and then another with Bonnie, and then Joyce and Margie. "What on earth?" Lisa had made sure I would be home because they all had planned to take me to lunch. Bob and Ed stayed home with Michael, and we went off to spend an afternoon catching up with each other.

Sitting around the table, they were all talking at once. I told them I wanted to know what was going on in their lives, and so I suggested that we could all hear better if we took turns one at a time. Well, of course, that got a huge laugh. They reminded me that I was still leading!

The Gold Jacket

When the announcement was made that Christa was among the candidates for the Teacher-in-Space program, we were all caught up in the excitement of Christa going off to Washington with 113 other teachers. What an adventure! Ed called our son Stephen, who was then living in Monterey, California. "But, Dad," he said, "she is only one of 114!" Then, thinking it over, he decided that to be one of the 114 selected from 11,500 applicants was really something. Charles Sposato, a teacher at Farley Middle School in Framingham was also one of the 114. Our son Stephen and Charlie had worked together at Farley, and Stephen had high regard for him. When Ed called Betsy, our youngest child, who lives in Venice, California, she was just plain thrilled.

Concord High School's principal announced that one of their teachers, Mrs. McAuliffe, had sent in her application for the Teacher-in-Space program and was one of the seventy-nine teachers from New Hampshire to compete in the program. Soon afterward, a student stopped her in the hallway and asked for her autograph. Christa gave it to him saying, "Whatever for?" After the first cut was made and Christa became one of the two delegates from the state, he came up to her and said, "See, it's worth more already!"

Christa enjoyed clothes, but she did not give them a high priority. She had an adequate winter wardrobe, but during the summer she lived in shorts and bathing suits. "Teachers don't need a summer wardrobe!" she said. Her husband admired her "Gibson girl" figure, but she found it a chore to shop and be fitted properly. Ed retired in 1985, so we had time to shop for some summer clothes for Christa to take to Washington, since she was busy with the closing of school, exams, grading, her children, home, and other activities. Ed had a good eye for clothes, we both enjoyed shopping, and we thought that a shopping spree on Christa's behalf would be fun. And it was. We brought up to Concord a selection of suitable and smart-looking dresses, and a gold silk jacket that was our gift to her. Christa's sister Lisa added her gift of a skirt and cotton knit top. Christa was wearing the gold jacket and Lisa's top and skirt when she was named Teacher in Space at the White House on July 19, 1985.

I became concerned that Christa was trying to do too much and would become ill. I tried to help in small ways; together we went over her clothes and accessories. She had everything set for each interview and occasion. We both felt that if she had all her outfits coordinated, it would give her a greater sense of ease and confidence and would mean that she had one less thing to think about. She was taking with her my new gold bracelet, inlaid with two rows of multicolored jade stones. Ed had bought it for me just that spring when we were in San Francisco; we had been told jade brought good health, and that was our wish for her.

We spoke on the telephone the day before Christa was to leave for Washington, and being a mother, I said again, "Get to bed early!"

The next morning, Christa called, "Just checking in before leaving."

"Are you excited?" I asked. "And did you get enough sleep?"
She responded:

Well, that's another story. I had the kids down and was finishing getting clothes ready for the week when the doorbell rang. A young girl in a highly agitated state stood on the porch. I knew her from school, although she has never been in one of my classes. I did know one of the teachers and a psychiatrist were working with her along with her parents. She was practically incoherent, and kept saying that she was going to kill herself. Quickly I had her come in. By promising she could stay with us, I finally got her permission to call her parents and her doctor. Since I had given her my promise, they agreed it would be best that she stay. Steve warned me that I had no authority to counsel her and there might be legal implications. "So sue me," I told him. By three o'clock, we were both bleary-eyed and desperately in need of sleep. She was calmer and no longer talking about killing herself. I put her to bed in Scott's room, in the lower half of his bunk beds. She would never try to harm herself while sharing a room with a child! This morning she left with her parents. I really think we made progress, but they all have a long way to go!

Later Christa called from Washington. She was having a wonderful time and thoroughly enjoying those of the 113 other teachers that she had met. The president spoke to them; the pilot from the January flight spoke to them. They were told about the dangers of the space program. She said that one could be intimidated thinking of all that he had said until you realize that NASA employed the most sophisticated safety features, and they would never take any chances with their equipment, much less an astronaut's life. And, no matter who was chosen as the Teacher in Space, all the finalists would be going to Florida in January for the liftoff. That announcement made the candidates enthusiastic; they were all part of the team!

She had run into Charlie, the Framingham teacher, and they jogged together early in the mornings. They encouraged each other and joked about the two of them coming from Framingham. "Maybe it's something in the water?" "Something in the air?"

Christa took time to visit teacher friends Pat Mangum and Donna Decker Thompson. Donna was to be married that fall, and Christa came up from Houston to attend the wedding. She had a great reunion with Pat and Donna, and with Carol Sharkey, who had taught with them before moving to North Carolina. The papers carried a story about their being together with a picture of Pat, Carol, and Christa arm-in-arm. Donna now has a little girl, Christa Marie.

Christa stayed in Maryland Thursday night with Pat and Donna, went shopping in Washington on Friday, and then flew from Washington to Manchester, New Hampshire, Friday night, all the time unaware that Terri Rosenblatt, the coordinator of the program, was trying to reach her on the phone.

The decision had been made early as to the final ten. Some of the candidates had been notified before they left Washington, and they were told to stay on. Christa arrived home at 12:30 A.M. Saturday. The phone rang at two A.M.; Steve woke from an hour's sleep and answered groggily. Calmly he handed the phone to Christa, "It's somebody from NASA. You've made the final ten and have to go back to Washington today."

There was little time between the second Washington trip and the date on which the selected teachers would report to Houston. When Christa arrived home again, one of the first things she did was to take all her travel clothes to the cleaners. She planned to pick them up on Saturday, put them back into her garment bag, and be all set for her flight to Houston on Sunday.

While out doing errands on Saturday, she made her last stop the cleaners. It was one o'clock. She tried to open the door. Locked! On the door there was a small sign indicating that closing time on Saturdays was twelve o'clock. No one was around. What to do? Reminding herself that there was no time to panic, she knew she had to find out who the owner of the store was and where he lived. She started by inquiring at the nearby stores, found out his name, and then where he lived. Her first few calls received no answer. Telling herself that someone must be home later, that they were only out shopping, and that they were coming back, she continued to call and finally made the connection. After she explained her predicament, the owner graciously said he would meet her at his shop and told her not to worry – she would have her clothes for Houston.

Because Christa felt so good wearing her gold silk jacket, she wore it for interviews and special occasions. She called it "lucky."

After the ceremonies at the White House on July 19 marking Christa's selection as the Teacher in Space, the press flocked after Christa as she was being hustled along the grounds to a conference. She answered what questions she was able to: "I'm still kind of floating." "I don't know when I'll come down to earth." "I am not an astronaut." "I am a space participant." "It's a positive step for teachers who need to feel good about themselves as a group." "I've always been thrilled about the space program." To questions about why there had been no blacks or Hispanics chosen, she replied, "The application process was totally color-blind." As far as political pull, applicants were told right from the beginning that any letters or phone calls asking for special consideration were automatically discarded.

A large color picture appeared on the front page of the newspapers showing Christa being hugged by David Marquart, the teacher finalist from Boise, Idaho. David told her, "Next time, I'm going to get myself a gold jacket!"

Grandmother and Christa

Ed's mother had been living with us for a few years before she died in February 1984. We took her back home to Waterbury, Connecticut, for burial beside her husband. Her nephew Father Jim Leary said the Mass and asked Christa to be one of the readers. Christa and her grandmother had always been very close. She received and wore her grandmother's platinum and diamond wrist watch. She was wearing it on January 28, 1986.

Christa went up to the altar to read and was doing very well when she hesitated, then stopped speaking. She tried to compose herself by putting her finger to her lips, tilting her head downward, and breathing deeply. After a few moments, she was able to continue.

When then Vice President Bush announced that Christa was chosen the Teacher in Space, and handed her a statuette of a teacher holding a child and reaching upward, Christa started to speak and the same thing happened. Watching on television, we saw her put her finger to her lips, look down, and, after a few moments, continue – it was the same response she made at Mom's funeral. As Ed watched her, he said, "You know, if Mom were alive right now, she would be thrilled, but she would say, 'Christa, this is just wonderful, but you can't go.'"

IV

Selection and
Preparation for Space:
1985-86

The White House

When President Reagan announced, "I'm directing NASA to begin a search in all our elementary and secondary schools and to choose as the first citizen passenger in our space program, one of America's finest, a teacher —"

These words opened the door to many adventures for Christa. One was an invitation to a State Dinner at the White House. This she turned over to NASA so the necessary arrangements could be made. When they neglected to respond she was embarrassed by a follow-up call from the White House: would she and Steve be attending the dinner? A friend asked me if I had received an invitation. I laughed and said, "When Christa is in the White House, I'll have plenty of invitations." I had no doubts that after she came home from her year of being the Teacher In Space she would teach a few more years and then go on to a position in school administration. There she would be better able to help cure some of the nation's educational ills. From there I thought she would be the right age and would have had the right exposure; and the country would be ready to accept a woman. As president.

Christa was a vocal New Hampshire Democrat. She admired Eleanor Roosevelt and the martyred Kennedy brothers, John and Robert. NASA had been asked to have her tone down her political views. At dinner, Christa was seated on President Reagan's left. Their conversation was nonpolitical.

They swapped stories, a teacher and a veteran of the movies. The president told her about his hobbies and life on his California ranch. Christa said they really enjoyed each other. When the entree was served, the president helped himself to two pieces of meat, leaning over to say to Christa, "I'm really not hungry, but if I take only one piece everyone will follow suit."

After dinner, President Reagan told Christa, "Now watch this." He stood up, and so did everyone else in the room. "I love it!" he said.

Many Hollywood stars were at the dinner, but the one that stood out for Steve was Raquel Welch. "When she was announced," Steve said, "It was like somebody turned the lights on; she's a stunning woman." Two people that evening were busy signing autographs, Raquel and Christa.

"Just being there was wonderful," Christa said, "I was just thinking coming back to Concord this morning – Steve and I were dancing at the White House last night!"

The Selection

Christa, always running late, dropped her application into the mail slot on the very last day that it could be postmarked and accepted. Then the videotape interviews of the 114 semifinalists were sent to Washington. These were viewed by the selection committee before the candidates left home.

The final selection committee consisted of seven officials who had studied the videotapes and the applications of each candidate. Now they needed to know which one could best promote the space program and handle the pressure, the time away from home, the media, the training, and the flight. Which one could talk to 10,000 people at the National Education Association convention and inspire them?

Ed Campion, NASA's media coordinator, summed it up, "We're not looking for Superman; we're looking for the person who can do the best job of describing his or her experiences on the shuttle to the most people on earth."

Christa's interest in trying to communicate the experience of flying came when she, Steve, and the kids flew to England aboard a 747 jumbo jet in the summer of 1984. "While we were on board and 40,000 feet up in the air, the children looked out the window. They were so excited that their excitement was transmitted to me. I want to be able to convey that to my students. So like a woman on the Conestoga wagons pioneering the West, I too would be able to bring back my thoughts in my journal, to make that a part of history." Christa easily transferred her exhilaration with flying to space flight; and like the pioneer women before her, she planned to keep a journal of her experiences in the shuttle for others to share.

We met Terri Rosenblatt, project director of the Teacher-in-Space program, when we were waiting for liftoff. Terri told us that they called Christa outstanding in a group of outstanding people.

Christa may have been the one who most clearly understood what they had in mind – she had done her homework. But as Christa commented:

You could put all our names in a hat, pick one, and it would be a good choice. But if a male had been chosen, I would have been angry. Each of the male finalists was articulate, attractive, and personable, but look back on all the teachers you've had in your life – who comes to mind? Historically, teaching and nursing are among the few professions that have not been dominated by men. If you're going to choose someone to represent teachers as a whole, I think you should be truly representative. You should choose a woman. I didn't get where I am because I worked a lot of years to achieve it or because I'm the best teacher who applied. I had a little luck and probably a judge or two pulling for me here or there, so I'll never see myself as *the* teacher or *the* perfect citizen because I'm not.

Christa told 12,000 employees of her former school district in a giant back-to-school assembly at Capital Center Sports Arena in Landover, Maryland, that she was their representative for the next year and that people all over the country would judge teachers by her performance. She promised to live by the rules that she set for her students. "I ask them to be themselves and to do the best they can. I figure if I follow my own advice, I'll represent you well."

Teacher-in-Space Announcement

It was a fun day. We all had good vibes about Christa being named Teacher in Space. She had come across strongly and seemed to be more focused than the others. But then you never know – *we* knew she was great, but would the judges know that, too?

That morning I did some errands, and then, to pass the time until the announcement was made, Ed and I decided to work in the garden around our patio. When the outdoor extension rang, I answered the phone to hear Colleen at Framingham's wkox radio station excitedly ask me what I was feeling.

"Slow down, Colleen. We haven't heard a thing. It will be on at one o'clock."

"Mrs. Corrigan – she made it!"

"But it isn't time yet – how do you know?"

Christa had told us that there would be absolutely no leaks to ensure that not even the one chosen would find out early. But the finalists rebelled at that. They protested that this was not a beauty contest and that they should be prepared beforehand. It was agreed that they would be told on the way to the announcement.

"Mrs. Corrigan – I'm telling you! She made it! I'm watching her on the monitor – she's crying."

Ed, seeing my reaction, took the phone, asking, "Are you sure, Colleen?" She was sure – yes. Now we knew, and it was wonderful! What joy Christa must be feeling. With each step of the Teacher-in-Space program, she delighted in the experience, and each experience made her yearn for the next! She wanted this so much!

A quick shower and change and we were ready to greet whoever came by. The first reporter arrived as our neighbor came running over. "I have CNN on, and they keep showing Christa over and over!" We had missed the announcement, so the four of us went next door. There we saw and heard her say, "You would never think that a teacher would be at a loss for words! I've made nine wonderful friends over the last two weeks, and when that shuttle goes up, there might be one body, but there'll be ten souls that I'm taking with me!" We felt so proud of her. Then a bird's-eye-view camera showed her walking to a car with a large flock of people swarming around her and after her. Ed laughed and said she looked like a queen bee with all her followers zigging and zagging after her.

Back home, the telephone kept ringing, the doorbell kept ringing, and cars lined up in the street. Lisa and Kit came home. Television crews set up their lights and cameras, photographers were snapping pictures of our pictures of Christa. When our photographer friend Art Marasco called from Lenox, I said, "You would just love this. I wish you could see all that is going on."

"Take some pictures!" he told me.

R. D. Stahl of Channel 7 started his interview on the evening news with Ed playing "You're Gonna Hear from Me" on the piano. When I spoke about Christa being a good choice, I called her level-headed. Christa, later seeing the tape, gave me a look and said, "Oh, Ma!"

I defended myself, "Well, you are."

We had not heard from Christa, but even if she had a chance to call, she probably would have reached a busy signal. We tried to call Steve, but we couldn't get through. We did speak to our other children, relatives, and a lot of friends.

Ed, Kit, and I planned to be at the Manchester airport when Christa's plane got in that evening. We would meet Lisa and Bob there. It was late, so we planned to stay over in New Hampshire and had to take our dog, Jessie, along. She was not allowed to ride in Ed's Grand Prix, so we took my Mustang. On the way, we stopped to buy a dozen long-stemmed American Beauty roses.

We worried that we wouldn't get there before the plane landed. We were late. Rushing into the crowded airport, we were greeted with cries of "You made it on time," "Her parents are here!" and "The plane is late."

We hugged Steve's mother, Rita, Steve, and Scott and tried to see relatives and friends. Congratulations were shouted, the air was filled with excitement – more than two hundred people were waiting for the Teacher in Space.

Seven-year-old Scott was born after the Space Age had begun, so he kept wondering what all the fuss was about. Steve tried to explain, "You can't just buy a ticket for a shuttle ride – this *is* a big deal!"

When the plane arrived, we were asked to stay inside while Steve and Scott went out to meet Christa. We could watch on the monitor as Christa stepped off and was hugged and kissed by her husband and son. There were a few other passengers on the plane, and they looked bewildered as they made their way through the normally quiet little lobby. Whatever could be going on? Music being played by bagpipers in costume, two people dressed as fat happy pigs dancing around carrying balloons, and a crowd restless with anticipation . . .

Christa greeted everyone as she made her way through the crowd. Finally she reached us, we got our hugs, and she got her roses. The media clamored after her. Such a hubbub, everyone wanted to be recognized. Christa was glowing.

For the twenty-minute ride into Concord, the police formed a procession, lining up the drivers in order. A police car led Steve driving Christa's van, and we followed. Relatives, dignitaries, and friends made up a long line that ended with another police escort. About five minutes on the highway we heard metal scraping and could see sparks flying. My muffler had come loose and was bouncing on the road. We would have loved to pull off the road, but fearing that those in back would follow us, we thought it best to stay in line, clanging and shooting sparks. How embarrassing – Ed commented, "We had to take *your* car!"

Lights were shining from every window in Christa's house. It was alive with people, banners, signs, and balloons spilling out over the porch and onto the lawn. Caroline was dancing up and down, waiting for her mother to get out of the van. Cameras were flashing. Everyone was exhilarated. The party went on as two happy children clung to their mother. There was so much to share, and Christa tried to talk to everyone. Finally, those not staying left for home – tired, happy, and proud. It was quite late. Ed and I slept in the family room on the second floor. We were awakened early the next morning by the sound of voices from the street. Looking out the window, I could see two police cars. The drivers were chatting to each other, and in the stillness of the morning, their voices floated up through our windows. A police guard had been stationed at the house, now they were probably changing shifts. The rest of the house was quiet.

Ed and I dressed and went downstairs. We had work to do. Christa had intended to have draperies made for the living room, but there never seemed to be time to choose what she wanted. For the interim, we had brought up with us enough pairs of lace curtains to fit her bay window and side window, and by using two pairs cafe-style, we could cover the eight-foot-long window at the stairway.

We found a stepladder and started to take down the curtains we wanted to replace. Lisa and Bob joined us. In no time, we had everything hanging except the curtains for the long window. The top was a problem. We poked the rod and curtains off their brackets with a long pole, but to get the rod with the new curtains back up into the bracket was a challenge. With the ladder set on the first landing, and Lisa and me holding it down, Bob put his left foot on the ladder and stretched until his right foot had a small hold on the middle sill of the window. Precariously balanced, Bob managed to jiggle the rod until it caught hold in the left bracket. Then with a pole and a lot of luck, the rod caught in the right bracket. Putting up the lower half wasn't difficult, and the curtains did look nice.

That fall, Ed and I chose some fabrics that we thought would be pleasing to Christa. During her next trip home from Houston, we met with a decorator at Christa's house and she decided what would look best. These were to be ready and hung before Christmas. In November, we were told the draperies would not be ready until January. Ed called the manager and explained that would never do, that Christa would be home for the holidays, and that it was important that they be hung – we had been promised. The manager understood, and the order was ready a couple of weeks before Christmas. Ed and I went to Concord to supervise the hanging. Christa's room looked elegant, and she was very pleased with the results when she came home. Thank goodness Ed insisted the curtains be ready – or she would never have seen them.

Now everyone was up and about. The house was buzzing, and the phone started ringing and just kept on. I took a call from Paris, a reporter wanting an interview. She was too late – Christa, Steve, and the children had just left for a press conference. There, Christa told reporters that "NASA has given me a book to read so I'll know a little about the shuttle. They are not going to put me at the controls – I know that!"

The Lions Club's parade was scheduled for that afternoon. They asked Christa if she would ride in it as the honorary chairperson. She asked me to help her decide what to wear, but solved the problem herself: "Of course – my flight suit and NASA cap!" Good choice!

Steve elected to ride ahead in the photographer's truck so that he could take pictures. That left a space in front with the driver, and I was delighted to sit there. Ed preferred to stand with Steve's mother, Rita, family, and friends. They gathered across from the Capitol building to watch.

Christa sat on the top of the back seat of a Mercedes convertible, her children alongside her. By the look of the crowds, all of Concord and the neighboring towns came to cheer. The people lining the streets waved, called out her name, and shouted all kinds of greetings and congratulations. Spirits soared during that ride. People ran to catch up with the car and shake her hand or give her flowers or take a picture. Christa waved back, called out to friends and students, and gave the thumbs-up sign.

Our driver, a young man, turned to me and asked, "What is this all about? Who is she anyway?" When I explained, he wasn't a bit impressed. "And I thought I was going to be driving Miss New Hampshire!"

The sun was beating down on us. It was hot and the children were getting restless. They tried to keep smiling and waving, but occasionally Caroline would droop. "When is this thing going to end anyway?"

The parade wound down at Memorial Field, where there would be speeches and contests. We didn't have to wait for those, but we did have to wait for Christa to meet various dignitaries and have an interview. Scott and Caroline were fidgeting in the car; they were hot and thirsty, and wanted to go home. A bystander noticed and generously brought over soft drinks. I was grateful and started to accept when they were politely pushed aside. "Absolutely nothing is to be given to the children except from family or with permission," I was told. Until that time, I was unaware of the security around us.

After the parade, Christa, Steve, and the children went off to the country club for a swim and a little private time. Ed, Lisa, Bob, and I went shopping to pick up some outfits for Christa to try on. We were successful and pleased with ourselves when everything fit and looked great. Now she was ready for the interviews that were coming.

This had been exciting, fun, busy, and tiring. When we reached home, we stopped to pick up a local paper, and there we were – filling most of the front page! The photo showed Ed and me holding Christa's wedding picture between us. Reality was setting in.

Some Family Reactions

Our son Steve is an assistant U.S. attorney in San Francisco. Before the launch, he was contacted by a local Massachusetts sportswriter about his thoughts on the publicity that his sister was receiving. The writer had covered Steve's sports career: three-time MVP in high school, three-sport all-star for the Bay State, and then football at Colgate. Steve had had his moment in the news, and now it was his sister's turn.

Steve recalled for the reporter the day at the Los Angeles airport when he glanced at half a dozen newspapers and "her picture was on the front page of all of them. I felt the temptation to approach perfect strangers and say, 'Hey, that's my sister!'" He continued:

I always liked my sister. I thought she was a good person – but to be in the public eye – no, I never thought something like that would happen. Christa always had a lot of enthusiasm, a positive attitude. I can't remember her being down. She always seemed to pick other people up.

When I found out she had applied with over 11,500 other teachers, I said, "Good luck to her." Then it came down to 114, and I started bragging. Now that I think about it, it's extraordinary. I have to re-evaluate her like never before.

I always had a healthy respect for Christa. She was the older sister and knew a lot more than I did. When she babysat, I paid attention to what she said.

We were friends and supportive. Christa went to my games, and I would go to the Marian High School games with her to watch Steve McAuliffe play. Later Steve and Christa would travel to West Point, Rutgers, and Colgate to watch me play college football.

I'll be in Florida in January for the lift-off. I'll have a ringside seat. I wouldn't miss it for the world.

Christa's sister Betsy, living in Venice, California, caught only the tail end of a television news story on the selection of the first private-citizen astronaut. When she heard the words "Concord, New Hampshire," she then knew her sister had been chosen as the Teacher in Space.

"I screamed and my cats went flying!" said Betsy. "It was a moment of exhilaration. It's funny, but when she first went out for it, I said, 'You have so much going for you, you're going to make it!' "

Christa had answered, "You're biased. You might think I'm qualified, but the people I'm up against are great."

Betsy has a bachelor's degree in sociology and has her own delicatessen in Palisades Highlands, California. Asked if she was worried about her sister's foray into space, she replied, "Worried? No way. Besides, I'm too thrilled to worry."

Emmy Awards

In the summer of 1985, Cable News Network named Christa one of the three heros of the year along with the stewardess credited with saving lives during the TWA hijacking and hostage crisis, and Lee Iacocca. Because of this, Christa was asked to be a presenter at the Emmy Awards for newscasters. She declined. She was going on vacation and said she did not fit a hero status. "A hero?" she queried. "A hero is one who has defied the odds by breaking a stereotype and endured the challenge of being first at something. Look at Margaret Thatcher. Whether or not I agree with her policies, the point is that she is a pioneer in her field. She's a good role model. My gosh, I haven't done anything. Ask me after I've flown." They persisted and even made arrangements for transportation to New York from the Connecticut beach where Christa would be vacationing.

The year before, Christa and Carol Bradley had planned to vacation at this beach with their children and had to cancel their plans. This year, Carol said, "Well, now I guess we can't go this year either."

"Why not?" Christa replied.

So the last week in August, they left for Hawksnest Beach in Old Lyme, Connecticut. Steve and Carol's husband, Ken, would fly down to spend weekends. During the week, Christa had a commitment to speak at the Concord Rotary Club. Ken flew his helicopter to the beach, took her to Concord for the Rotary luncheon, and had her back at the beach within a few hours.

Early in the evening of the Emmy presentation, a limousine was sent to the beach house for Christa and Carol. They were told they would have a room for changing, so they stayed in casual clothes for the long ride to New York, bringing their dresses and small bags with them. The driver dropped them off in front of the hotel. At the reception desk, Christa inquired, "Will you please tell me where I should go? I am one of the presenters for the Emmy Awards." They were given the number of the floor where the affair was being held.

No one was around to direct them after they got out of the elevator. Since it was late, they found a ladies' room and changed quickly, while celebrities came and went, looking at them with curiosity.

Coming out of the ladies' room, they passed an hors d'oeuvres table where they could see the remains of sushi and, ahead, the doors of the banquet room. Since there was no other place to get rid of their luggage, they tucked it under the skirts of the table and entered the room.

They found their places with the United Nations representatives, Joesph Kennedy, and his guest. Joe Kennedy told Christa that he admired her, and introduced her to everyone at the table. His friend turned to Carol and said, "I'm nobody."

"I'm nobody, too," responded Carol. They got along famously.

After a long evening of awards, Christa and Carol picked up their bags, which were still under the now-cleared table, and left the hotel. Their driver was waiting. He settled them into the limousine and took their luggage. He executed a sharp U-turn, taking their breath away, and headed out of the city.

When he asked if they were comfortable, they answered, "We're fine, but we're very thirsty. We'd love something to drink."

"Sure," he replied. "Where do you want to go? I can stop at any bar you'd like."

"No, no," they answered. "We're *thirsty!*"

"Oh, I gotcha. How about a McDonald's? One coming up."

When they pulled into McDonald's, Christa and Carol insisted that the driver join them. They had diet Cokes and hamburgers. Then, feeling satisfied and tired, Christa and Carol slept during the long ride back to the Connecticut beach.

Johnny Carson

NASA assigned Ed Campion as Christa's media coordinator. He set up television appearances, made appointments for radio, newspaper, and magazine interviews, and traveled with her to take care of all the details. Later when Linda Long was hired, she took over the scheduling. Christa's 1986 calendar rapidly filled with speaking engagements. Three commencement addresses were accepted for that spring: Framingham State (her college), Marian High (her high school), and Concord High, where she was teaching. One week that summer was blocked off for her to be in Bermuda. She was to speak twice there, and the rest of the time was for play. Steve and the children would be going with her.

Television talk shows were a wonderful setting for Christa's messages to students and teachers. She appeared on shows in California, New York, Boston, and Manchester, New Hampshire. One morning in New York, three shows were scheduled, each one on a different network. With Ed Campion's help and the services of a car and driver, she was able to dash from one studio to the next, making all commitments.

She particularly enjoyed getting out to the Los Angeles area because it was an opportunity to visit her sister Betsy. When Christa was to be on the *Tonight Show* with Johnny Carson, her brother Steve decided to drive down from San Francisco with his family. They would stay with Betsy and her partner, Angie. Angie's niece Gloria was going to take care of Steve's sons, Brian and David, while the adults were at the studio. Betsy and Angie were meeting Christa's plane and would be with Christa until the taping – so Betsy was to call Steve after he arrived at her house and give him directions. Steve and Anne were to get their directions, take Brian and David to Gloria's, and then drive to the studio in Burbank. The schedule was tight.

When Christa arrived at the airport and tried to claim her luggage, it was not there. Quite a bit of time was spent trying to trace it. When it was finally located, she was told it would arrive in a couple of hours. So Christa, Betsy, and Angie decided to have lunch while they were waiting. When the luggage arrived, Betsy brought the car around. Christa took the parking ticket saying, "I'll take care of this. I was told to keep track of my expenses and I will be reimbursed. So far, I haven't been and do I have a list! NASA is having trouble as to who is handling what."

It was much later than expected when they reached Christa's hotel. "I was supposed to call Steve!" Betsy suddenly remembered. She tried her house, but there was no answer. She tried calling her neighbors to see if Steve's car had been there, but no answers there, either. She called Gloria's, and the line was busy. Panic set in, and Betsy predicted, "If he drove all this way and misses the show, he will never speak to me again!"

Meanwhile, when Steve and Anne didn't hear from Betsy, they found Gloria's telephone number, called her, and drove to her house. They telephoned the studio for directions to the *Tonight Show* taping, and driving as fast as he dared, Steve fumed all the way. "Wait until I get my hands on that sister of mine!"

Betsy had at last reached Gloria and knew that Steve and Anne were on their way and that Steve was furious. She and Angie left Christa to dress, and they went to the studio parking lot in the hope that they would meet Steve and Anne.

Christa was taken to a dressing room that had her name on the door. A woman came in to make sure that Christa's nose wasn't shiny and to see if she needed any help. She was horrified to see Christa wearing a white suit. "One *never* wears white on television!" (Christa's blouse was bright blue, and she *and* the clothes looked great on the screen.)

Johnny Carson knocked on her dressing room door, and when he entered he said, "Well, I know who you are –," to which she replied, "And I know who *you* are."

A long line was waiting to get into the studio. Betsy described Steve and Anne to all those who looked official or helpful, and then started to jog around the parking lot looking for them. As she raced back a minute before the door would be locked, those still in line called to her, "They're inside – they're inside." Betsy just made it through the door.

Steve was surprised to find himself outside the studio gates with a few minutes to spare. However, he had driven up to a private gate and was unable to get in. Fortunately, a car pulled up, and when the driver entered his code and the gate opened, Steve squeaked through behind him.

On the program, Christa answered questions about her role in the shuttle flight and her training in Houston. After Christa had spent fifteen minutes on his show, Johnny Carson commented, "I think NASA made a very good choice. You are able to communicate this to most of us who really can't understand it."

After the show, Christa took her guests backstage for a tour, and then they exited to the back parking lot where Johnny Carson's green Mercedes and Christa's limousine were waiting. Several people were also waiting there for autographs. As Steve was watching his sister sign autographs while the driver of her car held the door open, he moaned, "And I don't have a camera!"

Later, when Christa was asked if she felt nervous on the *Tonight Show*, she laughed and replied, "I've handled children for fifteen years in the classroom; I can manage fifteen minutes with Johnny Carson."

Christa called us when they all got back to Betsy's. She said they were having a great time, and she laughed as she recounted all the mishaps. The taping had been at 5 o'clock, and they were going to watch the show when it went on the air at 11:30 p.m. I said, "I wish I had been there with you!"

Christa answered, "I've been invited back to host the show. You can come then!"

Houston Training and a News Conference

In an interview, Christa said that the day is long past since unmanned rockets exploded on their launch pads, since daredevil astronauts endured years of torturous physical conditioning and then hurtled through space in capsules the size of Volkswagen beetles. She continued:

People don't realize how big the space industry is. As teachers we have been a little remiss in looking at the program and saying there might be a job there for you someday. What is big now will get bigger – much bigger – in the coming decades. Scientific space stations are being constructed and as orbiting factories are built to take advantage of the weightless environment for the manufacture of exotic materials, eventually thousands of people will work and live in space.

A lot of people thought it was over when we reached the moon. They put space on the back burner. But people have a connection with teachers. Now that a teacher has been selected, they are starting to watch the launches again.

Ed and I attended the last 51 L *Challenger* team news conference in Houston. Barbara Morgan, Christa's alternate, and the students whose projects were elected to go into space discussed the lessons that would be taught from the shuttle. Barbara explained that her role was to be in Mission Control, in communication with Christa. Christa excused herself from this portion of the news conference and watched the interview from a monitor in another room, not wanting to be a distraction from Barbara's time with the press.

Then it was time for the 51 L crew to talk with the press. Dick Scobee, the mission commander, sat next to Mike Smith, the shuttle pilot, then came Judy Resnick, Ron McNair, Ellison Onizuka, and Gregory Jarvis; and at the end of the long table sat Christa. The press filled the room; cameras were all over the place. Dick Scobee said that "the publicity associated with this flight is a flash in the pan. When the next flight comes along, it will be forgotten. But the long-term effect is of raising the expectations of students that in their lifetimes they will live and work in space. If that expectation is there, it will happen." Judy Resnick, the flight's mission specialist and the other woman scheduled to make the flight, matter-of-factly described how she would use the ship's huge robot arm to launch the Spartan/Halley satellite designed to study Halley's comet. Greg Jarvis, the flight's payload engineer at Hughes Aircraft, spoke about the studies that he would conduct on fuel tank configurations for space vehicles. The news conference had the tone of a group of executives announcing a new product.

During all of this Christa was sitting so quietly that her father mentioned it. "I wonder if she feels okay?"

"Wait," I said.

When it came to Christa's turn, she looked as if she were spot-lighted; all animation and charm, her brown eyes danced and shone in the television lights. She said she planned "to look out the window a lot and experience the wonder of space and bring it back; I will be filming lessons and trying to stay out of the way. In fact," she said, "learning to avoid being a nuisance represents the biggest part of my training. I can look – but not touch!"

During the question period, the press kept directing questions to her, and then questions came over the wire from papers around the country. Christa loved it all.

The space agency press corps found it easy to understand why Christa was selected for this flight and why Barbara Morgan, an elementary school teacher from McCall, Idaho, was selected as her alternate and ground partner. Both women radiated friendliness and enthusiasm. Both had the ability to put an audience at ease. Both were quick with the quotable phrase.

For example, Christa said that it will be a "geography lesson" for her to see "how the world really looks from space" instead of on a map. "I grew up like half the kids in the country, thinking the states were different colors."

Barbara said that "ever since they first sent a chimp into space, I wanted to go." Barbara was to introduce the lessons broadcast from earth, giving viewers a brief description of the shuttle, updates of the mission, and the progress of the experiments. Then Christa was to introduce each crew member and explain their roles, show the cockpit with its 1,300 switches and dials, and explain how the crew members eat, exercise, and sleep in weightlessness. She would also answer live questions from students in the Concord and McCall schools where she and Barbara taught.

Christa's second lesson would be to explain how the shuttle flies. She would discuss why people explore space, report some technological advances created by the space program, and explain why industrialists were excited about manufacturing in space. Christa was also to film lessons on magnetism, chromatography, Newton's laws, plant growth in liquid solutions, and effervescence. These lessons would not be broadcast but would be distributed later to schools around the country.

Christa had to learn how to use the nylon sleeping bag and how to stick the cap from a tube of toothpaste to a strip of Velcro to prevent it from floating away. She had to learn how to cut the plastic tops off food packets and eat without letting the food float about the ship. Floating around the living area of the shuttle creates a whole new set of decorum requirements. At times, there would be five people working, exercising, making meals, or sleeping, all floating around in a small area, so it would not be unusual to be kicked in the head – it would be just one of those things that happens from time to time.

Christa's 114 hours of training in Houston for her space flight involved mastering thick training manuals and using teaching programs on a space agency computer. The instructors tried to give her an overview of how to live on the shuttle so that if you want to turn on a light, you know what switch to use. And if a warning light comes on – don't panic.

The Right Stuff

According to a journalist at the time, NASA's primary concern with the Teacher-in-Space program was to get today's pupils interested in the space program and the many career opportunities it offers. NASA would seed its pool of tomorrow's astronauts, scientists, and technicians, helping to ensure America's supremacy in space in the years to come.

NASA wanted to rekindle the excitement that once surrounded the space program by choosing a teacher who had the gift of gab. It had to be someone who could shake an apathetic public out of its torpor and get people excited about the space program again. That ability to get people excited, as it happens, is just what the best teachers have.

In public relations terms, the journalist went on, Christa could not have been a better choice. At thirty-seven, she was a good age, not too old, not too young. Pretty but not too pretty, with wholesome attractiveness, the sort of good looks to which ordinary people can relate. Her husband, Steven, a lawyer, was her high school sweetheart. She had two children, a good number – Scott, eight, and Caroline, five – good ages, and even one of each sex. And they were cute kids. Even the fact that she came from New Hampshire, where the presidential primaries begin, seemed politically perfect. Christa McAuliffe was as American as apple pie.

But with a good teacher's forthrightness, Christa was quick to set the record straight:

None of that mattered. We weren't even asked our age on the application form. There were no questions about family life. The selection process was totally nonpolitical. It was very refreshing. NASA was looking for a good teacher. It didn't matter how old you were or what you weighed or how you looked. They wanted a good teacher. Period. The rest didn't matter.

Christa in Houston

When Christa reached Houston for her NASA training, one of her greatest concerns was whether she would be accepted by the astronauts and their families. Her role was unique – she was the first private citizen to infringe on the astronauts' tightly knit core group. Her job as representative of teachers throughout the country would take much of her energy, and for her to be effective, she would have to be acknowledged as part of the astronaut team.

Her fears were partly dispelled after meeting June Scobee, wife of mission commander Dick Scobee. Christa said, "Mom, you will just love her. She understands where I'm coming from. She's a teacher – I can *talk* to her!"

When Christa arrived at the Johnson Space Center, she found it big – very big and impressive. She felt as if she didn't know one-hundredth of what was going on, and that became one of the messages she wanted to get across. There are thousands of employees, but what most people see are only the few astronauts getting on board the space shuttle. Yet lots of other things happen.

There was so much information and reading material given to her that she said she'd probably be sixty-two before she finished going through every last piece of paper that she would bring back from the Johnson Space Center.

When interviewed by *Space News Roundup,* a newspaper at the Johnson Space Center, she was asked to describe some of the reactions of her students, fellow workers, and friends. What happened when the announcement was made?

Christa indicated that she had received many notes and phone calls, and had a number of people stop by the house. She'd be out pulling up weeds or something, and kids would run up and give her a hug and say, "Oh, I can't believe it! This is so wonderful!" Everyone was excited, and she wished she could be back at school to share the excitement with the students. "It's going to be difficult not being at school and with the kids who had signed up for my classes. I sure am going to miss them all."

The *Roundup* reporter went on to discuss Christa's being thrust into the spotlight, meeting with government leaders, astronauts, and celebrities. And then the reporter mentioned that she had been described as a viable candidate for state and national office. Her response? "Oh, help!"

The reporter continued, "Wealth and fame are yours for the asking – parades, helicopter rides, important people – let's face it, if you wanted to, you would never have to go back into a classroom again."

"But that's the key," Christa replied. "I want to go back. You are talking to a teacher. I didn't choose my career so I could get monetary rewards. I never would have gone into teaching if that had been what I wanted! It's never been a major consideration. A year of this is going to be fun, and I'm enjoying what I'm doing. I see it as an extraordinary year out of my life. But for fifteen years, I've been a classroom teacher. If the Teacher in Space doesn't return to the classroom, then something is wrong!"

"But would you accept that somehow the equation has changed? You no longer fit the definition of average person – you are a public figure."

Christa answered that the definition hadn't changed, and it was all right to be a public figure because that way she would have success reaching people. "This is not seen as a stepping stone. When I go into a radio or television station, I am looking at everything that is happening, and I can't wait to tell my kids!"

Astronauts are not usually comfortable with the press and prefer to have as little to do with reporters as possible. Judy Resnick once told Christa, after she had been besieged by reporters, "You know, you don't have to put up with all that."

Christa answered her, "Well, you don't in your job, but I do in mine."

Asked by the *Roundup* reporter about her reaction to signing auto-graphs, Christa replied:

Do you know how many hall passes I sign at school in one day? It's very similar. It still is funny when somebody asks me for my autograph, because I never collected autographs myself. I think sometimes people must want a little piece to take away with them, and this way they can take your signature. I don't mind doing it, but it still surprises me. The first few times I was asked, I kept looking around to see who they were asking!

You want to hear the best one? When the Challenger had the problem back in the summer with the heat sensors on the engine and they had to cancel the launch, one of Boston's papers called me and asked me what I thought was wrong! And I felt exactly as I do when I'm sitting there in study hall and a student comes up to me with an advanced functions problem, and wants some help. They see you as a teacher who therefore knows everything. And the person on the phone was so funny. I said, "I have no idea. What has NASA said?" The reporter said, "Well, they think it's a thermostat kind of thing, but what do you think it is?"

When she was asked what impressions her flight would make on the average student in the average school, Christa responded:

There would be a basic awareness of the space program and some of the things that are available. As a historian, teaching history, I look at it as an opportunity for history teachers to perhaps incorporate a little more of the space program as a part of the curriculum. Very little is in the books, because you don't need a lot in the books, it changes so fast. Rather than using a shuttle launch in current affairs to say, well, another shuttle has gone up, they might teach about what is being flown.

The reporter asked, "But how would your flight help people under-stand what the program is all about?"
Christa replied:

I just got off the phone with a journalist from London. She told me that NASA should have sent a reporter up first! A journalist would have a farther-reaching impact than a school teacher! I asked her how many people she sees individually on a daily basis. Teachers have contact. I don't see kids once, I see them either for a whole year, or on a daily basis for five months. My message to everyone will be that space is for everybody. It's not just for a select group of astronauts. That's our new frontier out there, and it's everybody's business to know about space.

The reporter responded, "But space will not be a wide-open frontier, accessible to hundreds or thousands of people for several decades. Does that dull the message somewhat?"

Christa countered:

No, I feel it's accessible now. If you had asked me seven months ago what I was going to be doing in January, I wouldn't have told you going up in the space shuttle. Just having me fly is a very clear message that space is accessible. You're taking an everyday, ordinary person on board a space shuttle and flying her. It means something because we are teachers, and teachers are approachable people. Not everybody has had an astronaut in his or her life, but almost everyone has had a teacher.

Maybe some students will decide they want to become teachers. I am delighted that this year is going to be so special for education. Teachers who would never have gotten any press are now being featured. People who have gotten certain scholarships, or even are on an exchange program, all of a sudden find themselves in the paper. This has not happened before. [This same enthusiasm was evident in a letter Christa wrote to Sister Denesita at Marian High School: "This is going to be a wonderful year!"]

The reporter implied that her role would be easy. "You will be doing what is natural for you, which is just to teach –"

"*Just* to teach?"

"Sorry, poor choice of words."

Don't you think that there is a lot of pressure to make sure that your lessons are something that will stand up to attention by the entire country? Teaching is not a natural thing. You have to learn. You should have seen me my first year teaching. There's a world of difference between that and fifteen years later. You never reach a point where you feel totally comfortable with what you're doing. There is always something to learn, always a way to make a lesson better. No matter how much I prepare, sometimes I go into a classroom and something doesn't work right. Teachers are very flexible because of that. So don't tell me teaching is easy. I don't buy it.

Christa and Barbara Morgan found furnished apartments two doors away from each other on Peachtree Lane in Webster, Texas. They had a large, bright office at the Johnson Space Center not far from the offices of the 51L crew. They found Texas hot and steamy, but everyone was helpful.

On a visit to the Johnson Space Center, Steve, Scott, and Caroline toured the space capsules, saw the moon rocks, met astronauts, and ate lunch in the center lunch room. Afterward, Christa asked Caroline what she liked best. She thought about it for a moment and said, "The tuna fish sandwich."

"It helps bring you back to earth!" was Christa's comment.

Ed and I went down shortly after their visit, and again Christa showed off her new surroundings. The evening of our arrival, the spouses of the 51L crew were hosting a tea for the spouses of the *Columbia* shuttle crew who had just gone into quarantine. The party was at June Scobee's home, and we were invited to join them. There we met June, Barbara Morgan, Jane Smith, Lorna Onizuka, Sheryl McNair, and Sally Ride, whose husband was in quarantine.

We met Christa after her workday and stopped in the office where the rest of the crew was winding down. We sat with them as they talked about their children or their music. We laughed with the crew when we discovered that all their children were excited about the trip to Florida for the launch – because they would get to go to Disney World!

When we were to leave for home, Christa asked if we could take two large packages back for her. "I have just so much to bring home for Christmas I don't know how I can manage them." She brought the packages out and then decided she should tell us what they were. "They're the presents for you and Steve – my official NASA portrait."

With tongue in cheek, she told us how she and Barbara went in to see their pictures when they were ready. The photographer had the pictures enlarged and framed. They decided that they really ought to buy the pictures, but they were so big! Whatever could the two teachers do with them? So Christa and Barbara decided that they could give the pictures to their husbands and parents, who would have to accept their gifts!

We managed to get the packages home and were delighted with Christa's portrait. It now hangs over the fireplace in the living room, next to the children's picture that they gave us for our twenty-fifth wedding anniversary.

Flights on the T-38 and KC-135

Christa called her flight on the T-38 aircraft exhilarating. The speed of the plane produced a force 3.5 times the force of the earth's gravity. "You felt like you were melting into yourself, like the Wicked Witch of the West."

Dick Scobee explained that "the primary purpose is to put her in a stress environment, in a situation she's never been in before. Speed, helmets, confined to a cockpit. It's not your everyday airplane ride, and if it bothers you, you probably are not ready for space."

Dick wanted Christa to experience as much as possible and kept extending the G-force until Christa wrenched her neck. They decided to keep it a secret since it wouldn't do for the press to find out that the mission commander had given the Teacher in Space a pain in the neck. A video was taken later of Christa being taught how to handle food during the shuttle flight. She is holding her head stiffly, and at a slight angle. I smile when I see that film, because I know why.

Christa radiated excitement when she talked about her rides on the KC-135, a hollowed-out 707 airliner with padding on its walls. The big plane headed out over the Gulf of Mexico and flew in a series of thirty to forty parabolas, climbing and diving. With each dive, the occupants experienced about thirty seconds of weightlessness.

"Oh, it's great. I love it," laughed Christa as she floated to the ceiling, grabbing Barbara Morgan's hand so they could strike a sky-diving pose.

Barbara hopped over Christa shouting, "The first leap frog in zero gravity!"

"We were at first trying to be very serious," Christa said later. "I said to Barbara, 'Let's get acclimated on the first parabola. Then we can see how our classroom experiments will work in zero G.' But it was hard to stay serious. Leap frog? Why not? We figured kids would love to see that. But there were these serious NASA people there. I don't think a lot of them would leap frog on a KC-135."

Christa's most important lesson was to learn where to go to get out of the way if something went wrong. Despite all the emphasis and training that the astronauts had in solving malfunctions, Christa felt no anxiety about the flight. "I don't see it as a dangerous thing to do," she said, pausing for a moment. "Well, I suppose it is, with all those rockets and fuel tanks. But if I saw it as a big risk, I'd feel differently." No American, she pointed out, had ever been killed or seriously injured on a space flight.

Asked if it would be difficult for her to return to her classroom in Concord after receiving national attention, she replied, "I don't think so. This is the first year since I was in kindergarten that I have not been in school. I really miss it. I miss the classroom. I miss the students. I miss the subjects I teach."

Barbara, speaking at a presentation, said, "I hope that when people see Christa in space, they won't want to become astronauts; they'll want to become teachers."

"The separation from family is tough," Christa commented. "Steve is doing a super job with the kids. I told him I would nominate him for parent of the year when this is over. You can see he would really like to be in my shoes, and he's vicariously thrilled."

Letters from Houston

This week has been quite an experience. I still can't put people in the right places with all of this bureaucracy. Not only do you have headquarters but there are also the administrators at Johnson Space Center. It's been fun to watch all the politicking that goes on.

Barbara and I found a nice apartment. We're sharing one right now, but her unit will be ready in a couple of days. It's a top floor apartment, cathedral ceiling with a sun room, one bedroom and bath. The living room area has a fireplace. The view out our back is a big lawn and lots of trees.

I'll be home Friday, September 20, the same day that Steve is leaving to go to his VMI reunion. I think I'm going to stay at Carol's. The kids were planning to be there anyway because Steve was going away, and I think I'd be better off not going home right now.

In a later letter Christa wrote:

We did get a chance to ride in the T-38s – a high altitude jet, and Dick let me have the controls and do rolls and dives. Mike Smith took Barbara up and she got to do the same.

I'm flying to Dallas tomorrow – helicopter to the airport and then Lear jet up to Dallas. A dairy company (a rather large one, but it is Texas) gives out five $10,000 awards to teachers yearly. I'm being asked to hand out the awards.

I also get to make a quick presentation – about ten minutes – about what I have been doing. (In ten minutes?) Jack and Judy Sheedy live in Dallas now, and another of Steve's college roommates, Dick Shellhammer and his wife. They have all been invited to the dinner so I'm looking forward to getting together with them.

Caroline started hockey last weekend. Steve said she looked so cute he was almost in tears. She wouldn't take a chair to help her skate. She went around the rink on her own. The piece of equipment she felt most proud of was the cup!

Steve took Scott to the Patriots' game last Sunday, and Scott had a wonderful time. He is such a creature of habit. They have been to two or three games before, so Scott insisted on tailgate parties and tossing the football around in the parking lot before the game because that is what they had done the other times!

Christa, Steve, Scott, and Caroline were guests that fall at one of the Patriots' games. During intermission, the team lined up to get Christa's autograph. Scott stood right alongside of his mother. After she signed her name, Scott would hold out his program to get each player's autograph.

"I'm still enjoying this different life," she wrote. "Thank God for Barbara, though. We both agreed that if we were doing this solo, we wouldn't last. We get a chance to relax and put things back in perspective when we are away from 'the Center.' I do not like the weather – so humid that breathing seems impossible at times."

Questions from Students

That fall, the *Concord Monitor* did a special supplement titled "A Student's Guide to the Space Shuttle: Christa's Challenge." The newspaper asked students in the Concord schools what they would ask Christa if they had the chance, and then they called Christa to get her replies. These are some of the questions and answers:

Q: Can you blow hard through your lips almost like whistling and propel yourself backwards?

Christa: I'm not sure. We tried it on the KC-135 but it didn't work. We'll try it again on the shuttle. Greg Jarvis doesn't think you can propel yourself by blowing, but he does think that holding a balloon and then releasing [the air in it] should move you across the deck. We will try that.

Overleaf: Wedding, August 1970.
(Photo courtesy of Art Marasco)

Wedding portrait, August 1970:
Leo and Rita McAuliffe, Steve
McAuliffe and Christa, Stella
Corrigan, Grace and Ed Corrigan.
(Photo courtesy of Art Marasco)

Christa dancing with her father at
her wedding, August 1970.
(Photo courtesy of Art Marasco)

Aunt Carrie's 90th birthday, Maryland, January 1975.

At home, 1977: Steve McAuliffe, Lisa, Steve Corrigan, Kit, Christa, Ed, Grace with Scott, Betsy.

At home in Concord the day after Caroline was born, August 25, 1979.

Christmas at home, 1979: Stella Corrigan with Caroline, Christa, and Grace – four generations.

Christa and the children on vacation, 1980.

First get-together with Jean Bain Sanborn at Carolyn Bain Bunick's house in Danvers, Massachusetts, August 1979: *first row:* Christa with Caroline, Jeremy and Josh Knight with Joyce Eklund Knight, Carolyn and Jenny Bunick; *second row:* Anne Donovan Malovich with Erica, Grace, Jean Sanborn, Bonnie Bain Finnigan with Katie; *third row:* Carrie and Sarah Bunick, Jamie Knight.

Concord Parade, July 20, 1985. The New Hampshire state capitol is in the background.
(Photo courtesy of the Concord *Monitor*)

Christa says good-bye to Concord High School before leaving for Houston and training, 1985.
(Photo courtesy of Concord *Monitor*)

NASA portrait of Christa, 1985.
(Photo courtesy National Aeronautics and Space Administration)

Christa and Barbara Morgan watch a shuttle liftoff in Florida, fall 1985.
(Photo courtesy National Aeronautics and Space Administration)

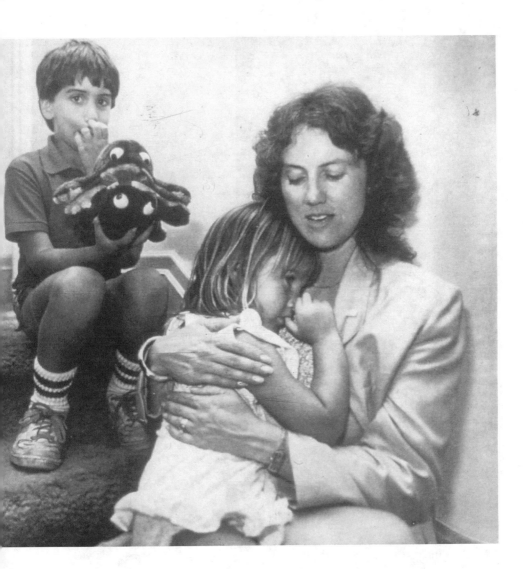

Christa and Grace on the Florida beach the week before the launch.

Evening before the launch, January 27, 1986: Grace, Betsy, Anne, Steve, Kit, Lisa, Bob Bristol, and Ed. (Photo courtesy of Art Marasco)

Christa with Scott and Caroline before the launch.

Dedication of Christa's House, Camp Wabasso, August 1988: Grace, Caroline, Ed, and Lisa. (Photo courtesy of Patriots' Trail Girl Scout Council)

Scott stretches – almost!

Caroline, summer of 1991. (Photo courtesy of Art Marasco)

Q: How does it feel to suddenly be a celebrity?

Christa: It's fun. The media experience is new to me, but I'm enjoying meeting lots of people and getting an opportunity to see "behind the scenes" at the TV and radio stations.

Q: Are you having second thoughts about doing this?

Christa: I get more excited about the trip as I do more of the training with the crew. I'm sure the adrenalin will be flowing when I'm blasting off!

Q: Have you tried any of the space food?

Christa: The space food tastes good. We have cookies, dried fruit, pudding, and granola bars which look just like the food you put in your lunch box. The meats and vegetables resemble the frozen foods in the boiling pouches that you buy right at the store.

Q: Why do you think you were chosen?

Christa: I'm not sure why because any one of the ten finalists are enthusiastic, good teachers who love their jobs and are very interested in the space program. I'm delighted that NASA chose me."

Q: What is the temperature in space?

Christa: Very cold and very hot. The temperature ranges from minus 275 degrees Centigrade in darkness to plus 275 Centigrade in sunlight.

Q: Which experiment do you think will be the most interesting?

Christa: The magnetism demonstration is exciting. There's a big, clear plastic cube with an electromagnet in the middle. When Barbara Morgan and I took the magnet up in the KC-135 to test it, the pattern around the magnet was wonderful.

Q: What are your fears about going on the space shuttle?

Christa: I truly do not have any fears. I'm excited about the trip and am thrilled to have the opportunity.

Q: Will you share your journal when you come back?

Christa: My journal will allow me to have good recall of everything that I'll be experiencing. I'm hoping to share these thoughts with as many people as possible when I return.

Q: What one thing do you want to discover up there?

Christa: Personally, I'd like to see how I do in a close, weightless environment with six other people. I'm not going with any preconceived ideas so that I won't ignore anything that happens.

Q: What would happen if you got sick in space?

Christa: Since you are in a weightless state, you need to use a bag and close it up quickly. Many people do not feel very well because there is a fluid shift – you feel bloated and there is no up or down. This nausea is gone in one to three days.

Q: What did you like least about your training?

Christa: There's nothing that I don't like. Everything is new and fun, and remember that I'm getting ready for the ride of a lifetime!

Christa and Her Students

When she began her training in Houston, Christa sent her Concord High School newspaper weekly updates of her activities, including NASA pictures of herself and Barbara Morgan. Concord High School displayed the pictures in a trophy case in the main hall. As the launch approached, Concord High School installed TV sets in every classroom so students could follow the action.

When the space flight was scrubbed because of a jammed bolt in the hatch door, the crew had spent five and a half hours lying flat on their backs strapped in their seats. Christa then wrote to her students: "Go borrow a motorcycle helmet. Lie on the floor with your legs up on a bed, and stay there for five hours. You can't read; you can't watch television. You're strapped down really tightly with oxygen lines and wires coming out of your suit. You can hardly say anything. Just lie there and you'll know how it feels."

A college recommendation that Christa had written for student Matt Mead arrived the day of the explosion. Matt, who has now finished his college years at the University of New Hampshire, commented, "I always remember Mrs. McAuliffe telling us how important it is to go out and experience new things. It's scary. Even if it means moving away from the people you love and care about, she said, you have to do it. She helped me understand that."

Neil Harmon, another of Christa's students, credits Christa with inspiring him to become a teacher. He reports that several other high school teachers had discouraged him from pursuing a career in education: "They were all down on it. But when I talked to Christa about it, she got really excited. And the last time I talked to her, she said, 'No matter what happens, keep going. Stick with it. It's really worthwhile.' That helped me persevere through the hard times."

Christa's students called her an inspirational human being, a marvelous teacher who made their lessons come alive. Mary Jo Drewn, seventeen and a senior at Concord High when she was a student in Christa's last course on the history of American women, called her "tough but fair – she gave a lot of homework, but we learned about stuff in history that was never brought out in the history books."

Yet Christa was no plaster saint, and she enjoyed telling the following story on herself – at her first back-to-school night at Concord High School she confidently told a group of parents that she'd be willing to answer all their questions – and then was unable to give directions to the music room.

A Prelaunch Interview

With her infectious enthusiasm, Christa made the launch of the *Challenger* a new experience from the stiff ritual that such events had become; in a typical response to a question from a *USA Today* reporter who asked what it was like to be an astronaut, she exclaimed: "It's neat."

Further in the interview, Christa went on,

I'm not sure how I'm going to feel sitting there waiting for take off and those solid rocket boosters ignite underneath me and everything starts to shake.

It's kind of like the first time you go on a carnival ride. You've said, "I've got enough courage," and you're really excited about doing this and conquering your fears. The training is not physically rigorous. Mentally, it is. You learn things so that you can understand the shuttle. But it's not like I have to figure out how it was put together.

The crew is unbelievable. Very professional. Very concerned about how I am fitting in with them, trying to make me part of the team. I'm amazed when you sit there and listen to them. Judy Resnick, for example, has a doctorate in electrical engineering. It's mind-boggling that she knows all these circuits and can figure all of this out.

Not only will I be teaching my lessons and doing activities, but I'm also helping. It's going to be fun.

I've talked with my kids about seeing the launch – some astronauts' kids have had bad reactions. I think they'll be okay. Caroline is six and Scott is nine. They are a little bit more aware of rockets and how they behave. Caroline doesn't like loud noise, so I told her it can be loud and that bothers her.

I was delighted that a teacher was chosen as the first space participant because there are so many of us who have daily contact with people. To think that teachers were finally recognized as the good communicators they are.

I'm hoping that everybody out there who decides to go for it – the journalist in space, the poet in space – whatever the other categories, that you push yourself to get the application in. I'm hoping there are going to be more people down the road who are going to apply for it. When you think of the future, there are going to be more people going into space, and they are going to be the kids who are in our classrooms. It's a wonderful thought."

Linda

Ed and I met Linda Long when we were at the Cape waiting for Christa's launch. She was with her mother and dad, and we all went out to dinner. Linda has remained part of our lives.

When Christa was selected as Teacher in Space, Linda was working as a "loaned executive" from the Gulf Oil Corporation to the staff of Frank Johnson, then the director for public affairs at NASA. In September 1985, Linda established her own public affairs, government relations, and political consulting business. Linda later wrote:

I never had the opportunity to tell you both what knowing your daughter meant to me. Shortly after beginning my firm, NASA asked me if I was interested in providing services to Christa. I can't begin to tell you how thrilled I was to be given the opportunity. Not only was Christa to be my first client, I was going to be a participant in one of the space program's most historic events – the first citizen to fly in space!

The only thing left to do at that point was to obtain Christa's approval. After all, she was going to have to put up with me on a daily basis for several months, and she had to make the final decision. The day I was to meet with her in Houston, the plane was late, the rental car stalled ten times between the airport and the space center, and I looked like I had been standing in a sauna by the time I rushed in to see her. This is just great, I thought. She is going to be really impressed with me all right! Will she accept me on the spot, or say that she has to think about it? Much to my relief, she overlooked my tardiness and disheveled appearance and welcomed my assistance.

Linda was to learn that Christa was always running late herself. Once when Christa and Barbara Morgan were dashing to get to a press conference and Barbara was fretting because they were late, Christa told her, "Slow down, Barbara. After all, it can't start until we get there." And as for appearances, the kids at Concord were used to Christa's hair not being dry until the end of her second-period class.

According to Linda:

Working with Christa was not just a job, it was a joy. I felt a special sense of duty to Christa. She was taken out of her home, away from family, friends, and school, and thrust into a totally new environment. The astronaut training, the NASA culture, the press, and the public interest in her every move were all new to her. Lots of different people and organizations were vying for her time and attention. Through it all, she never lost her sense of humor, her compassion for others, or her identity. She learned how to operate within the system and made it clear that she was no one's pawn. She was all business when it came to the project. She had a great sense of purpose and exhibited total dedication.

My duty was to interface with NASA and the outside world on Christa's behalf. I felt very protective toward her. I worried when her flight schedules were being toyed with, when she went out for a jog at night, and when she tooted around Houston Christmas shopping.

Last October we arrived at the Cape late at night to see her first [shuttle] launch. At about 11:30 p.m., I called her room to check if everything was okay. No answer. Called again. No answer. *Panic.* Went down to her ocean-front room. No answer at the door. Off in the distance, I heard laughing. I found her with Barbara Morgan and Judy Garcia on the beach in their bathing suits. I proceeded to tell them how late it was and that they had to get up early in the morning. What did they think they were doing? Didn't they know how dangerous it was to be running around the beach at midnight? Christa flashed that wry smile of hers and said, "Who do you think you are? my mother?"

Christa was the kind of person you loved to be around. She was so easygoing, with lots of vitality. She gave me energy. I didn't spend as much social time with her as I wanted to. I felt it was better for her to spend her free time studying, calling home, getting to know the crew, and so on. We would spend lots of time together after the mission, and I didn't want to impose. How I regret that decision today . . .

Linda wrote about being at the launch. "And then my heart broke. Not this launch, please not Christa. I felt as though somehow I had failed her. She was my responsibility. I was supposed to protect her."

Souvenirs

Soon after their arrival in Florida, Kit and Betsy were in the souvenir shop at Cocoa Beach filling up shopping bags with Teacher-in-Space T-shirts, hats, mugs, and buttons for themselves and to take home for gifts. When they came back to show us what they had bought, Ed and I went over. It felt odd to walk up and down the counters and see Christa's face on so many different items and to see so many people buying these things. We were told that business had never been so good and that they had already restocked three times. We bought some Teacher-in-Space patches and envelopes with the crew seal. Those we were going to address and have sent postmarked on the day of the flight. We took each other's picture outside standing in front of the large Teacher-in-Space souvenir sign.

Beach House

Ed and Marvin Resnick, Judy's dad, developed an instant camaraderie based on their mutual fathers' pride in their daughters. While Marvin took some snapshots, Betty Resnick and I chatted. We were all a little nervous waiting in the hallway for a doctor to examine us. A clean bill of health was needed in order to have a farewell lunch with the crew. The seven members of 51L were in quarantine, and every precaution was being taken to keep them free from any ailment that might delay the launch.

Kathy Krause, the commander's daughter, came out of the doctor's office crestfallen. She had a slight fever and was denied permission to go to the luncheon. We tried to console her, but that increased our anxiety as to how we would do. The doctor asked if I had any rashes. That was close – I often have one somewhere. Luckily, I was honestly able to say no. Great! The rest of us passed.

The next day, we were driven to the Cape and taken in jeeps to the beach house, three miles from the launch pad overlooking the Atlantic. It was a beautifully clear day, a little cool. The house was set off by itself, the beach and water were peaceful, calm, and lonely.

We had arrived early. The Resnicks, Ed, and I decided to take a walk along the waterfront while waiting for our astronaut – and "teachernaut" – children.

Betty Resnick wanted me to understand Judy's position as an engineer and astronaut, and I, in turn, wanted her to know that Christa would be a team player and that her dedication was to education. She would never pretend to be an astronaut. Christa admired Judy. She found her talented, dedicated to her profession, and impatient with any interference, such as the media. Walking back, we saw a small figure dash out of the beach house, look up and down the beach, and head for us. Among my fondest memories of Judy is her racing across the sand, black hair flying. She looked like such a little girl as she hurled herself into her father's arms.

The picnic luncheon passed all too quickly. The spouses were remaining for a longer visit. Ed kissed Christa goodbye, and as he turned to leave, she hugged and kissed him again.

We were walking down the steps of the deck to the car when he murmured, "It's almost as if she didn't want me to leave."

Receptions

Traditionally, astronauts host a reception the day or so before the flight for their guests who have come to witness the launch. However, since the astronauts are in quarantine, their families represent them. The receptions take many forms: lunch, brunch, tea, or cocktails and hors d'oeuvres.

June Scobee asked Christa if she would like to combine their parties. Christa was pleased and asked me to work with June on deciding the hotel, decorations, and food. I was still in Massachusetts and knew very little about Cocoa Beach and Orlando, so I was glad to rely on June's judgment. When June suggested putting a collage of photographs of our absent hosts on easels near our tables, it sounded like a great idea. I started to gather the appropriate pictures of Christa, from her baby pictures to her official NASA portrait. I packed them into the trunk of Ed's car along with poster boards, tacks, and tape.

The reception was to be a grand party, held in Orlando. We would get a chance to see our friends and relatives who had come to Florida for Christa. A cousin of mine called and said my aunt was so excited that she had already bought three different outfits and was in a quandary about which to wear.

The afternoon of our reception, NASA had scheduled appointments and interviews for Ed and me at the Space Center. These took much longer than we expected, and we were dependent upon a driver to return us to our condo so that we could get ready for the Orlando gathering. We had originally planned to arrive at the hotel early, set up our table and easel, and then have time to relax with June and Marcia Jarvis, who was joining us with her party.

By the time we reached our condo, we found that with over an hour's drive to Orlando, if we wanted to arrive on time we would have only ten minutes to change and get on the road. That took care of my primping!

We arrived at last, a few minutes late. As Ed pulled up in front of the Holiday Inn, Betsy dashed down the steps to the car and, taking the keys, removed the pictures from the trunk while I was getting out of the car. "We were worried that you were in an accident!" she gasped.

Ed parked the car as we hurried through the doors into a jammed corridor. "Why is everyone waiting out here? Why are the ballroom doors closed?" I asked. "Mom," Betsy replied, "our table is the first one as you enter, and Mrs. Scobee didn't want anyone in until we were all ready!" A pathway was cleared for us with a few cheers that we had finally arrived.

Lisa and Betsy quickly helped me set up, and the doors were opened. Ed and I stood at Christa's table, Ed proudly wearing his huge Teacher-in-Space button with Christa's picture. We greeted so many people; some we hadn't seen in many years.

Joanne Connor Brown, Christa's friend since college, came through the line with her husband Rick, her father and Rick's parents. Mr. Connor was quite pleased with himself, showing us Christa and Steve's wedding booklet. Joanne's in-laws lived in Maryland; when Christa and Steve sold their home in preparation for their move to New Hampshire, Christa and Scott stayed with the Browns until the holidays so that Christa would not have to leave her students until the end of the semester. (Steve had already left to start working in the attorney general's office in Concord and was using our house as home base.)

After the last guest had been greeted, we went to the podium. June Scobee then greeted everyone and spoke about the launch. We still had not had definite word as to whether it would be the next day, as scheduled. When June turned the microphone over to me, I just said that Christa sent her greetings and hoped everyone was having a good time at her party.

The mood was very upbeat. A cousin of mine who had come in from Omaha and whom I hadn't seen in twenty-five years walked around saying "unbelievable" over and over and shaking his head. Reporters and cameramen filled the hallways, catching interviews with guests wherever they could.

That evening was also the night viewing of the *Challenger*. We had been given seven tickets. Those who were going had to leave the reception early. Again we were on the run, facing the hour-plus drive back to Cocoa Beach where the buses were waiting. As soon as we arrived and boarded, the bus was off to the launch site.

As we drove up to the site, everyone became quiet, trying to see out of the bus windows to the large expanse of darkness and the brilliantly lit shuttle surrounded by individual lights.

We left the warm bus and gathered in a long line to stare out at the spectacle, each with our own thoughts. The night was very cold, and our breath hung in the air. My fur jacket felt good. Lisa had on a light jacket, and Betsy wasn't wearing any wrap. But the cold wasn't going to keep them from experiencing this excitement.

Ed and I held hands as we stood looking out at the glowing shuttle with lights twinkling all around. It all seemed unreal. Was this really happening? Was our daughter going to be strapped into that? The butterflies were starting.

V

After the Launch:
1986 to the Present

Framingham State College Memorial

On January 29, 1986, we arrived home from Florida. Framingham State College had already scheduled a memorial program for Christa on January 30 at noon. At first family consensus was not to go. "No one will ever expect to see us!" Linda Long, Christa's public relations official who had generously returned to Massachusetts with us, called the school to say that we would not attend.

That morning, I began to feel uncomfortable about not attending. It *was* Christa's school, and also mine. I could understand how the rest of the family felt, and I certainly didn't want to impose my feelings on them. But when it was almost too late to go, I turned to my son Steve, "I'm going. Will you come with me?"

We hurried to change, asking Linda to call the school and say that we were on our way. Ed said, "If you are going, then so am I"; the other children joined us as well.

At the school, the police escorted us to the back entrance of Dwight Auditorium where Governor and Mrs. Dukakis and College President and Mrs. Weller were waiting to greet us. Then we were led up the back stairs into the stage wings. The ceremony had been held up about fifteen minutes. I expected to be sitting in the front row of the audience. Instead we were in the front row of the stage, facing a completely filled auditorium. People were standing at the back and along the sides. After dressing so quickly, I hoped that I looked presentable and had all my buttons buttoned.

Many familiar faces were in the audience. The audience was very subdued. We were touched to see so many people. Dignitaries of the school and state spoke. Teachers who had an impact on Christa's life spoke. The music was directed by Professor James Savas, and was particularly touching, as Ed and I had attended many of his concerts, especially when Christa sang in the choir.

It was right to have been there, and yet I had to remember the last visit, in the joyous excitement of the previous fall's homecoming events . . .

Framingham State College's Homecoming '85 theme, "It's out of this world," celebrated Christa Corrigan McAuliffe, class of 1970, who would be the first schoolteacher on a space shuttle. But Christa's Houston schedule wouldn't allow her to be at the homecoming, so I was asked if I would do the honors of crowning the king and queen in her place. I was hesitant, though pleased. A mother instead of an astronaut? Would the kids buy that?

The day began with a dedication ceremony for the new College Center, named after Framingham State President D. Justin McCarthy, who was retiring after twenty-four years of service. Dr. McCarthy had handed Christa, Kit, and me our diplomas; he had played a major role in continuing the physical and academic development of the nation's first public teachers' college, founded in 1839 by Horace Mann. Dr. McCarthy played a major role in the lives of his students as well.

A noontime parade followed the dedication. As parade marshals, new President Weller and Mrs. Weller and I led the line of floats to the homecoming football game. The weather was soggy with rain off and on. We watched the game from an enclosure as the players slipped and slid around the muddy field.

At halftime, President Weller and I went to the section of the field where the coronation ceremony was to take place. The young people gathered around, their spirits high. I was still feeling a bit out of place until the president introduced me: "Christa could not be here today because she will soon be going out of this world, so we have with us her mother, who brought Christa into this world!"

Well, that got a burst of laughter, cheers, and applause. I was welcomed warmly, and the ceremony went off nicely. Yet little did I think that day when I was playing a small role in the college festivities, that this was only the beginning.

Homecoming was in October, and in November Christa was invited to be Framingham State's commencement speaker at graduation in 1986. President Weller's invitation read, "You have given the class of 1986 a lifelong incentive and something truly historic to share. In many places around the campus we see and hear the sky is no longer the limit for Framingham State students. As you know, such an aspiration is difficult to instill in students (or people, for that matter). We thank you for it."

Since Christa was going to carry something on the shuttle from Framingham State, Professor Stephen Durkee of the art department designed a flag, and from that design medallions were made. These Christa McAuliffe Medallions are now given in award programs. Kit presented the first medallions on January 17, 1986, to three major prize winners from 900 high school history students across the state just before he left to join us in Florida for the liftoff.

Johnson Space Center Memorial

Johnson Space Center in Texas was to hold a memorial service for the Challenger Seven on January 31, 1986, at eleven o'clock. We were called the day before and asked to be there early. Linda Long became busy on the telephone trying to find transportation to take twelve of us to Houston.

The Xerox Corporation generously offered their company jet. It was just becoming light when the State Police arrived to escort us to Bedford Air Force Base, where we boarded the plane. Once airborne, everyone was rather quiet with their own thoughts and with trying to keep their emotions under control. I was worried that Steve McAuliffe's sister Melissa was not eating and that our son Kit was withdrawing into himself in his difficulty in accepting what had happened.

Landing at Ellington Air Force Base in Houston brought back memories of being there with Christa. There she had shown us the huge KC-135 known as the "vomit comet" that the astronauts used to get accustomed to the feeling of weightlessness. We had admired the slick T-38s that Christa had flown in so many times with Dick Scobee. Propping up her camera, she had taken her own picture while training in a T-38.

We were driven to the NASA Building at the Johnson Space Center where the families were waiting for President Reagan to arrive. Besides officials of NASA and ninety-seven astronauts, many of the ten thousand workers at the Space Center were waiting on the vast lawn. Linda had arranged the seats; Ed and I in the second row, behind President and Mrs. Reagan, and the rest of the family a few rows back.

Everyone stood as the president's party walked out of the building for the service and came down the steps to where they were to sit. Mrs. Reagan walked directly over to me, put her arms around me, and said, "You have lost a beautiful daughter." She kissed Ed. The president shook our hands and offered condolences.

Later we received a letter from the president dated January 31. He wrote, in part:

Her loss, which has been so hard for all of us who knew her primarily through images and press reports, we know must fill you with terrible anguish. Your Christa, like the other members of the Challenger crew with whom she perished, took upon herself the hopes and vision of an entire nation. She more than represented the teachers, the wives and mothers and the loving daughters of this land; she epitomized them. She was the best of us, a sign of the finest things the human spirit can become. But we know that there is a special way in which only those who brought a child into the world can grieve. And though we cannot take away any fraction of your sorrow, we can say that Christa is loved and missed by all of her fellow citizens.

That day, the president spoke eloquently about sharing the loss of seven great Americans who had led their lives and lost their lives in honor. He bade them good-bye, saying, "We will never forget you."

Suddenly to the right, four NASA T-38s appeared flying one thousand feet over Johnson Space Center in the Missing Man formation. Just before they were above us, one plane left the other three, zooming ahead, faster and higher. Emotions were released, tears flowed.

The families then regrouped in Building 19, and we had an opportunity to speak with each other. When speaking to Jane Smith, I commented on how well she was holding up, and she answered, "Mike would be furious if I didn't." Jane is such a pretty woman with a delightful wit and a way of coming out with the darnedest sayings. She would crack us up. Once, talking about her dog, she said, "You know he belongs to me because we wear our hair in the same style and color."

Lorna Onizuka was having a difficult time. I had talked to her before the service, and then Ed and I sat with her for a while afterward. She couldn't be comforted.

Senator Edward Kennedy sent a message to us. He, Caroline, and John would like to pay their respects if we wouldn't mind meeting them in another room. After greetings, Caroline said, "Your daughter was an inspiration to me." To which Ed replied, "And your father inspired Christa."

Memorial Masses

Christa's memorial funeral Mass was Monday, February 3, at St. Peter's Catholic Church in Concord, New Hampshire. Cardinal Bernard Law, Archbishop of Boston, and Odore Gendron, Bishop of Manchester, presided. Christa's cousin Father James Leary was the celebrant, and the priests of the parish, Father Chester Mrowka and Father Richard Lowes, were concelebrants. Watching them and the many other participants proceeding down the aisle, I thought, "My goodness, Christa! This is all for you!" How many times since then I have had the same thought.

Steven McAuliffe asked me to do the first reading. Walking to the podium, I prayed, "Come on, Christa, help me through this." I chose Proverbs 31: 25–31:

Strength and honor are her clothing; and she shall rejoice in time to come. She opened her mouth with wisdom; and in her tongue is the law of kindness. She looketh well to the ways of her household, and eateth not the bread of idleness. Her children rise up and call her blessed; her husband also, and he praiseth her. Many daughters have done virtuously, but thou excellest them all. Favor is deceitful, beauty is vain; but a woman that feareth the Lord, she shall be praised. Give her the fruit of her hands; and let her own works praise her at the city gates.

As I stepped from the podium, I missed my footing, but caught myself before falling. There was a collective leaning forward of the congregation and then a collective release of breath. How Christa would have appreciated the humor amidst the solemnity!

Carol Bradley read the responsorial psalm. Carol and Christa had become close friends when they were both teaching at Bow Memorial School, Christa's first teaching job in New Hampshire. Later, when Christa was dashing about for NASA, Ken Bradley often flew Christa into the Boston airport in his helicopter. Jennifer, their daughter, babysat for Scott and Caroline.

Anne Donovan Malovich, Christa's friend since childhood, had the second reading. Her lower lip wouldn't stop quivering as she sat waiting for her turn. She focused on one of the priests at the altar, who had been their classmate at Marian High, and tried to will herself not to be nervous so that he wouldn't notice. When Father Leary left the altar to share the handshake of peace with us, he hugged me, saying that I had given him the support to carry through the Mass. I answered that if I hadn't been the first reader, I probably would never have been able to read at all.

Steve wrote a beautiful eulogy for Christa, which was delivered by Michael Callahan, Steve's law partner and a close family friend. "She came into class late," wrote Steve, "and I knew I had to meet her."

Two days later we were at St. Jeremiah's. There our children did the readings, and Barbara Kelly Tupper read a tribute to her childhood friend. "And, yes, I was jealous, but then I'd remember that this was Christa, and that made it all right." We had lived next door to the Kellys for seven years when we first moved to Framingham.

Steve asked if Ed and I would go back to Concord with them. "Of course," I replied. "How long do you want us?"

"How about ten years?"

Ed and I packed some things and went to Concord with Christa's family.

Back in Concord – The Mail

When we got back to Concord, Steve and the children stayed on the second floor and gave Ed and me the newly finished master bedroom. Walls had been knocked down on the third floor to make one large room and a bath with a jacuzzi and skylight. The bedroom was bright with the draperies that Christa had just finished hanging during the Christmas holidays.

Scott and Caroline went back to school. The three of us were left to make some sense out of all that had happened. No mail was coming to the house; it was being delivered to a room in the Concord police station, so mail became a priority.

We went to the station to see what the situation was. The room looked like a post office. Trays of mail were stacked upon long tables set against one wall. Trays were stacked under the tables. Packages of all sizes and shapes were piled against a wall, almost reaching to the ceiling. Large cartons on the floor overflowed with manila envelopes.

We decided to plunge in; Ed and Steve began to read letters and I slit open envelopes with an electric opener left for our use. We hadn't made much headway with one tray before another delivery of more trays and cartons arrived. At this rate, we would not make a dent.

I started to develop a system as they went through the mail. I labeled trays and cartons as the categories emerged. Trays were set aside for personal mail, contributions and other donations, mail from friends from Framingham, Concord, Virginia Military Academy, Marian High School, Framingham State College, and so on. On the floor, the cartons were labeled Mass cards, letters, sympathy cards, notes from children, and schools.

We worked about three hours each day. After three days Steve gave up in frustration, saying, "Do whatever you want with it!" Ed felt that he really couldn't handle any more either, so it was time to accept the help that was being offered. Margaret Lind set up a schedule for Christa's friends to work at the police station. While they worked on the mail, I started to tackle the packages. Each item was given a number, and I kept a record of the gift with the name and address of the sender. We worked one, two, or three hours a day for a couple of months. Steve chose a printed reply card from those that NASA had sent for his selection, and I asked NASA to send us copies of Christa's official portrait to be sent with our replies to children and schools. NASA agreed. The NASA cards and envelopes arrived by the thousands, giving us plenty to work with, but delivery of the pictures and their envelopes was erratic. Sometimes the pictures would come, and we would wait for the envelopes, or envelopes would be addressed and we would wait for the pictures.

Ed was back home in Framingham, so I would go down to see him weekends. There our family had sorted out the bulk of the early mail sent to us. There was much left to be answered, and more was coming in. We kept up the best we could. Once Ed handed me an envelope, saying, "Imagine receiving this." It was from a midwestern state and addressed to Mr. and Mrs. Edward Corrigan – nothing else.

The mail from children was wonderful. It came singly or in packets from a classroom. They wrote poems and drew pictures. They told Scott and Caroline to try not to be too sad, and how they, too, had cried. They wrote in innocence, and we laughed to read, "My teacher is making me write this." Or, "My teacher is *not* making me write this." Some told us that Christa was only lost and would find her way home. One little boy said he watched the liftoff with his class, and it spoiled his whole day. Another wanted to be a teacher, but "it's too dangerous!"

Some letters were so poignant that they brought tears to our eyes. So many started with, "You don't know me, but I had to write." A mother of a social studies teacher sent an article that her daughter wrote:

But it was the loss of the teacher-in-space that magnified the gut-wrenching emotion that I experienced last Tuesday. It has taken me a while to sort out the feeling. But as I watched person after person, all across America, from every walk of life, of every age, color, and creed, seemingly consumed with the same kind of grief, I began to comprehend. We had all lost a friend. (*Glens Falls, New York*)

Perhaps I'm too emotional, but I can't get her out of my head. Smiling, waving, and throwing herself into it with contagious enthusiasm, and suddenly gone. (*Idaho Falls, Idaho*)

I owe it to Christa for helping me find a foot-hold in my own goals and dreams. I can only say thank you to her parents for the influence she had on my life. What an honor to be in a profession where courage and determination have never been shown any better than the way your Christa showed them. (*Arkadelphia, Arkansas*)

We have met many times on the 'Evening News,' and I feel as though she was part of our family. Unfortunately, the media has suddenly declared her some kind of a special hero because of the recent tragedy at Cape Canaveral. While I completely agree with their conclusion, it is for a different reason. Christa was indeed, both special and a hero, long before she entered the space program, not because she dared to reach for her star and suffer this tragedy, but because she dared to make this a better world through sharing of herself in educating our young people. If hero be the label [for] special people such as Christa, then let it be for the tremendous wealth of good that she did during her life rather than for her tragic death. (*Gibsonia, Pennsylvania*)

Sharon Newman, a Teacher-in-Space finalist, wrote:

I knew that I was going to be the first teacher in space . . . And when the name McAuliffe was picked instead of mine, I said, you have made a mistake – It has to be me! And, as the *Challenger* lifted away from the launching pad, can you imagine what went through my mind? I was supposed to be there instead of Christa McAuliffe! And then it happened.

There's a lot of work to do down here – touching kids. I also know she's cheering me on – every time I eat a peppermint ice cream cone [our favorite], wear my apple earrings [hers went down in the shuttle], or sing "You're Gonna Hear from Me" . . .

Nicki Wenger, one of the final ten, wrote shortly after Christa's memorial Mass in Concord:

Christa was a sister to me and very special. Part of me went with her on that shuttle – just as she said it would – and part of her is still with me. We had a bond and we shared an excitement for something that few people outside the family circle can understand or comprehend. Being there at the services surrounded by the warmth and love of her friends and family was so comforting and helped me immeasurably to deal with what happened. You will always be family to me. Christa had a dream and a goal and I will do everything in my power to carry it on for her and for you.

She will always be remembered as the first Teacher-in-Space – she did accomplish that goal. She also is having a very profound impact on education – and I know she's looking down on us and saying "Neat!" Don't be afraid for others of us who will fly and carry on her banner to reach for the stars. It's a passion that is beyond words and Christa would have wanted us to continue the mission for her and for the kids as well because we want to – now more than ever. We are the brothers and sisters she left behind who will always love her and you."

On March 1, 1986, I received the following letter from Judith Maloney Boyle:

I was Christa's sixth grade teacher at Brookwater School and I remember her well and fondly. She was a sunny, lively, excellent student. I did not realize Christa McAuliffe of Concord, N.H., was also Christa Corrigan of Framingham until after the tragic event. In the years since we were teacher and student we had gone different ways, grown into different people. I happened also to be a New Hampshire resident, and cheered for my neighbor and fellow educator when she was chosen to be a teacher astronaut. As she trained and prepared for a voyage into space I and all Americans were stunned and speechless when the mission failed . . .

It was Mrs. Corrigan I recognized on TV. Somehow out of the recesses of time and memory I felt I'd met you before. And then the name echoed – Christa Corrigan, Christa Corrigan, and finally the face of a little eleven-year-old girl came to me – smiling, eager, bursting with joy and energy. It was midnight when it clicked and for the next hour I rummaged through boxes and books in the attic until I found her in a class photo taken on the steps of the Massachusetts State House on field trip. Then I truly knew I had taught and nurtured Christa for a time, and I felt proud.

A thirteen-year-old wrote that she had agoraphobia and had thought of killing herself. "But I'll look at Christa's picture and remember how brave she was and decide to be brave myself. She gives me strength to go on." She wrote many times after that and kept us posted about her progress:

I'm so much better now . . . I am so happy. I never could have made it through without Christa's inspiration. It's so hard to explain why Christa is so special to me but, her spirit helped me through so many hard times – I did so good in school this year, not only for me, but for Christa.

Another letter read:

Christa McAuliffe was a gentle woman of grace who displayed all the virtues of humanity, courage and self-sacrifice, but most particularly, it was so beautiful to see how this great lady inspired the school children of our country. I thank you for providing her to all of us. (*Haverford, Pennsylvania*)

From the mother of a teacher:

When the tragedy occurred, my daughter vowed she would teach. She has been teaching for a year and a half now and already a blind girl realizes that the only thing she is unable to do is see; a Viet Nam veteran is finally finding a way, through education, to put his life back on track; and a young woman who barely made it through high school is now pursuing a four-year college degree. It gave me a great deal of pride that my daughter chose to be a part of what she calls "Christa's team" – carrying on for Christa. Her first week in teaching, she wrote a note to herself that sits on her desk. It reads, "I touch the future; I teach for Christa and for me." (*Berryville, Arkansas*)

From the People's Republic of China came this letter:

I hope you could find some consolation at the thought of the brilliant achievements your daughter has left for mankind. She was not only a loss to you, but a loss to the people of the whole world. She will never be forgotten by us all who admired and respected her.

A letter from Cambridge, Massachusetts ended:

Christa valued personal journals and diaries very highly for their insight into the minds and experiences of the common people. She made a commitment to write a journal as a legacy for the American people. We must now take up this task for her, and all the tasks in this life that she can no longer finish, having been called to something higher. Like any good teacher, her directions are clear.

From Coldwater, Michigan:

Every space launch was a family television event. She was flying for me. She would be my eyes and ears and her exploits would be mine. Her achievement was more significant [for me] than Sally Ride's because I could never be like Sally, the astronaut; but I could dream of being like Christa. Perhaps that's the one reason her death hurts so much: we mourn not only the loss of Christa and her crew, but also the small part of ourselves that died with her – our hopes for her success, our anticipation of her return, our dreams of glory.

From Portland, Oregon:

I smirked cynically, certain that the teacher-in-space was just another expensive public relations ploy meant to appease and distract the American educators from the real problem: lack of federal support for teachers. I began to take interest in Christa McAuliffe in spite of myself. She reminded me of the ideals that had moved me to become a teacher in the first place. And, yes, she did make me feel proud to be a teacher again. To Americans, space shuttles had become an ordinary occurrence, and education had become blasé as well. McAuliffe reminded us that space flight was a miracle and that teaching was no ordinary endeavor, but can be a miracle, too. Christa can't return to the classroom, but I can. Tomorrow I'll stand a little taller. I'll strive a little harder to achieve my dreams, and I'll encourage my students to reach for theirs. McAuliffe has reached her dream; her mission is accomplished.

From Holden, Massachusetts:

Your loss has become the loss of people everywhere, and a loss to me in personal terms I never dreamed possible. I never met your daughter Christa, but her personality beamed out through her work this past year, and I felt like I've lost a friend I've known for life. I never heard your daughter speak in person, but I followed her interviews and her words of enthusiasm, spunk, determination, and drive made me smile, and now help me through this tragedy. I never had your daughter in a classroom, but I believe that her contagious joy and love of life, which she so eloquently expressed in her very act of living, taught me lessons I will never forget. Christa's sudden death, so unexplained, so unexpected, has taught me the most important lesson of all: Life must be cherished, loved, and lived every moment possible, and pushed to its fullest. Christa did that, and in doing so, truly became the teacher-in-space. We honor her most by following in her footsteps . . . It's a tribute to Christa that so many people who never knew her believed that she carried and represented their dreams and hopes for the future.

One afternoon, after reading letters for about an hour, I threw up my hands in exasperation, startling those around me. I wailed, "Christa, will you just look at what you left me with!" And then I laughed at myself because I knew she would have given her standard response – "Now, really!"

Recently, I have been reviewing some mail and found that a few things were overlooked. One was a check made out for a scholarship fund. I was embarrassed by the oversight, but, fortunately, I was able to reach the sender. I was not so fortunate in the case of a woman in Iowa who sent a dollar. I'm sure that dollar meant a great deal to her. I could not find a telephone listing, and the note I sent was returned "forwarding order expired."

The packages held all sorts of religious articles, bibles, Korans, crucifixes, rosary beads. Books to console, to inspire, to make one laugh. Tapes and videos of memorial services and songs, stuffed animals large and small, and, with a great deal of mail coming around Valentine's Day, lots of candy. Beautifully crocheted and sewn pieces, dolls, quilts, and pillows were unpacked. Cards, some as tall as I, were decorated and filled with hundreds of signatures from schools, towns, cities, and offices. Proclamations came from across the nation, some in envelopes, some on scrolls, and some framed. Pictures of Christa and the shuttle were in pencil, poster paint, water color, crayon, charcoal, and pastel – small and large, framed and unframed. Even with the best intentions, I worry that we have missed acknowledging some of the gifts.

It was near the end of May before we began to see the end in sight. Dozens of boxes had been sealed, labeled, and put into Barbara and Mike Ruedig's attic, just across the little park from Christa's house. What was left, Margaret Lind and the others would handle. It was time to clear out of the police station; it was time for me to go home.

Even now, letters come in. Some are familiar; some are writing for the first time. My hope is to display the mail from schools, publish the poems, and – wouldn't it be great? – have an art exhibit of the children's work. When the Christa Corrigan McAuliffe Center is completed at Framingham State College, these archives will have a permanent home.

Telephone Calls

We have had our share of obscene and harassing telephone calls. Steve McAuliffe kept a recorder on his telephone and put in a second line with an unpublished number. Ed and I were not at our home most of the time to be bothered. Some of the callers would ask for Christa, some demanded to know what was wrong with us, and then there would be the one who would play a recording of Christa's voice. These finally dwindled away, but there was one that stayed persistent.

After Ed returned to Framingham, he called me in Concord, very upset. "These calls are driving me crazy. I can't take much more of this. Tomorrow I'm going down to the telephone company and get our number changed."

This troubled me. We should be forced to change a number that we had had for thirty-five years because of someone like that? I wanted to catch whoever was doing this and try to stop the caller before he or she went on to the next victim. "Hang on," I told Ed. "Don't let it get to you. I'll be down Friday night and take over the phone for the weekend."

The previous month our telephone bill had logged over twenty collect calls in error since none had been accepted. We had a record of where these calls came from. Ed took it with him when he went to the telephone office and gave it to the service representative. He explained about the calls. Our phone would ring and an operator would ask, "Will you accept a collect call from Christa?" Before anyone could speak the caller would yell out, "Oh, that's right – she blew up!" or something to that effect. The offender sounded like a young girl. Three or four of these calls would usually come in over a period of an hour or so. Ed was distressed, and the service representative was in tears.

Before having our number changed, the telephone company decided to put a tracer on our line, but that would take a while. Until then, the supervisors in the areas of the numbers that appeared on our bill were alerted. These came from pay stations in Boston, one near a police station. The supervisors were asked to have their operators transfer any collect calls coming in for our number. Then the supervisor would try to hold the caller on the line while notifying a police car in the area of the call. They hoped to catch the caller in the telephone booth. This gal was busy. She'd switch from booth to booth without being seen. Can you imagine someone wasting their time like that?

The calls trickled off and then finally stopped – to our relief. Apparently, the game became too dull or having a supervisor interrupt some of the calls made it less exciting. Or perhaps she found another victim. Whatever it was, I wish we'd been able to take some action. She needed help.

Dealing with the Media

After the explosion, the family had all agreed not to give personal interviews, and the media was usually very understanding. At various times they would call, but there would never be any pressure when the answer was no.

Our son Christopher (Kit) worked at Framingham State College, where he was continuously surrounded by memories of his sister. The college held ceremonies on the first anniversary, which attracted quite a lot of media. Many reporters kept after Kit to give a statement.

At home that night we turned on the six o'clock news. There we saw Christopher Corrigan being interviewed at the college. He was saying that in his opinion NASA used his sister.

A short time later Kit arrived home. "We were just watching you on television," we commented. He replied that he felt he had to say something.

His father answered, "We all do what we feel is the right thing."

Me, a Speaker?

Early in 1986, we had a decision to make. Who was going to deliver Christa's commencement speech at Framingham State? The logical choice would be her husband, but Steve felt that he wouldn't be ready by then to speak in public. And would I be? We finally decided if Steve could, he would. If not, I would.

As the date came nearer, I decided that I'd better start to draft the points I wanted to make. I asked Steve if he was going to help me.

"What have you written?"

I showed him my notes.

"Where's your outline? You can't write a speech like this! You need some structure — where is your beginning, middle, and end?"

"Steve, I'm not a writer or a speechmaker. I'm putting down everything I want to say, and then I'll put it in order."

"Well, I'll work on it and see what I can do."

I was more than willing to let him have my notes. I knew he could do much better than I, and that was important since we were doing it for Christa.

When Steve had finished putting the speech together, Ed and I went to his office to do some editing. He had done a great job, but it was much too long. With the help of the computer, we went to work, changing what we thought needed changing and deleting what we felt we could do without.

Steve was supportive of my making the presentation. "It's your school," he said, "do it. Read it a few times, not too many. Before speaking, take a deep breath and take your time. I'll see you there. Good luck!"

The speech was still too long when we timed it at home, so Ed and I made more cuts until we got it down to twenty-five minutes. Then we decided to leave it alone. Ed was still concerned. "Nobody will want to listen to you that length of time!"

But they did. They gave me a tremendous reception. I know Christa was pleased.

The woman sitting behind Ed commented, "I could have listened to her all day."

Ed turned around and said to her, "Lady, you darn near did!"

Christa was given an honorary degree which Steve accepted.

Getting her doctorate was one of the things she was hoping to do in the next four or five years. It was sixteen years ago almost to the day when I sat very much like you in Virginia waiting to receive my degree. And I think that most of you, from what I can see, have the same three wishes I had that day. I wanted to get my degree, I wanted to get out of town, and I wanted a beer. So I won't hold you up one second longer except to say thank you very much.

Framingham State College created the Christa Corrigan McAuliffe Center for Education and Teaching Excellence to honor Christa and education, and seven permanent scholarships have been established. The mission of the Center is to carry out educational activities and research that will support teachers in their work and improve educational practice, to offer students goals and incentives to enhance their development, and to strengthen community support for public education.

Another feature of the Center is an exchange lecture program between Framingham State College and Bowie State University in Maryland, where Christa earned her master's degree.

The first annual dinner was held in Boston. Senator Edward Kennedy was guest speaker and urged the audience:

> The legacy of Christa McAuliffe should be a nation committed to excellence in education and in the fight against illiteracy. Illiteracy in America is a national disgrace. We may not be able to halt crime, end poverty, or cure disease, but at least we should be able to teach our children how to read.
>
> Christa was a gifted teacher, a woman of tremendous vision, courage, and appeal – and we were all her pupils. Christa McAuliffe touched us all in much the same way President Kennedy did. He would have loved her enthusiasm and her enterprise because it was the spirit he saw in his own frontier. Now, like Jack, she belongs to the ages. They both will be forever with us, challenging all of America.

When it was time for me to speak after the dinner, I thanked all those attending the dinner, but stumbled over the word *excellence*. Needing help, I appealed to those sitting on my right and saw everyone at the head table leaning toward me, their lips enunciating "ex-cel-lence." When I corrected myself, I think 800 people gave a collective sigh of relief and relaxed. A video had been made of the television coverage that evening, and we were watching it later at a committee meeting. On one of the stations a young woman commentator flubbed *excellence,* prompting the remark from one of our committee members, "It's catching!"

Ed Remembers His Daughter

During Alumni Weekend in June 1986, Framingham State College awarded Christa their Alumni Achievement Award. We had been asked to accept the award for her, and I asked Ed if he would like to give the acceptance speech. He gladly accepted since he felt that he could give an insight into what Christa was really like through a few examples of their father-daughter relationship.

After thanking the college and accepting the award, Ed started talking about their times together:

Back in 1961, when Christa was thirteen years old and a very busy baby-sitter, I stopped at a local jeweler's to pick up a watch that had been repaired. The shop was displaying a handsome silver liqueur set of six cups and a tray, and I was quite impressed with it. I asked the price, and when I learned that it sold for thirty dollars, I knew that no one with five young children and my income could afford such a luxury. That evening, I mentioned it at home, and my wife agreed with my decision to forego the liqueur set.

A week later, I stopped into the jeweler's again to take one more look to see if I should splurge and buy it. The jeweler advised me that it had been sold. I left, musing to myself that it was probably just as well. The following Sunday was Father's Day, and, as you have probably deduced, Christa presented to me, by using her savings from babysitting, the gift I coveted – the silver liqueur set, which remains one of my prized possessions.

In late winter 1969–1970, Christa was a senior at Framingham State College and was looking forward to the Senior Dinner Dance and to her fiancé Steve McAuliffe's arrival in Framingham to escort her. Ten days before the dance, Steve called from Virginia Military Institute where he was a senior to say that his company was going on field maneuvers for a week and he would be unable to attend the dance in Framingham.

Christa was disappointed, but she just made another decision. The following evening at dinner, she said she really wanted to go to the dance and asked me if I would take her. I was flattered to be asked but questioned what her peers would say when she showed up with her father. Even then Christa was confident in who she was – she said her friends would think it a great idea, and she knew we would enjoy it because I liked to dance more than Steve did, so she would have more time on the dance floor. She was right! We had a wonderful time!

More recently, in the fall of 1985 after Christa had been selected for the Teacher-in-Space program, we were together in Framingham at a family celebration, and for a moment we two were alone. I was so taken with her success and how beautifully she was handling her celebrity that I said, "Christa, do you know what? You're wonderful!" She countered, "Dad, do you know what? So are you!"

Later, at the second annual fund-raising dinner for the Framingham Christa McAuliffe scholarships, Ed was the keynote speaker. He remembered keeping in touch with Christa by telephone during the last few days before liftoff. "During one of those calls, Christa told her sister

Lisa that she was delighted to hear that Mom and Dad were thoroughly enjoying being the parents of the Teacher in Space. She said she felt she had added a new dimension to our lives – and she had."

Ed then spoke about the various new dimensions that we were experiencing:

The most immediate new dimension brings me before you this evening. My plan is to give you my personal view of Christa McAuliffe.

In the summer and fall of 1985, I was often asked, "How does it feel to have your daughter chosen as NASA's Teacher in Space – and were you surprised when she was chosen?"

How did it feel? How does one describe practically indescribable joy? Knowing how much Christa wanted this – that she termed this the ultimate field trip – the day she was selected was one of the greatest days of my life.

Was I surprised? Yes. Although Christa had always been special to me and her family, even I was surprised when, from a field of ten impressive and wonderfully talented finalists, NASA judges unanimously chose Christa on their first vote. Being chosen as a space participant was a demonstration of Christa's strong and independent spirit. She was always striving to be the best she could be, stretching the limits of the system and never accepting the status quo.

In 1966, she showed her independent spirit when she wore the first strapless gown ever to grace a Marian High School Prom – much to the chagrin of the school's administrators.

This spirit of independence accompanied her to Houston where she went for her space training. Christa wanted to teach the lessons to be televised from space *her way,* not NASA's way. Each lesson would last only twenty minutes as the shuttle passed over the Caribbean within range of a tracking and data relay satellite orbiting 23,000 miles above the coast of Brazil. So there was little margin for error. NASA wanted the lessons to be scripted. Christa did not. She said, "This isn't a stage play. Teachers don't need speeches. All they need is a lesson plan and students. It has worked for ages on earth, and there is no reason why it shouldn't work up there." NASA relented. It was done the teacher's way.

Christa was a warm, sensitive, loving daughter, and I, a proud father.

Steve Speaks to the NEA

Speaking to the National Education Association convention on July 4, 1986, Steve McAuliffe said:

Of all the groups in America that Christa hoped to benefit she was most concerned about you, her fellow teachers. When the Teacher-in-Space program first began, many people, even those in your own profession, were skeptical. Educational institutions reacted almost instinctively: if it was an Administration-sponsored program, it must somehow be bad. At best they thought this program was a feeble substitute for desperately needed help – substantive material help – for the educational system. And at worst, it was thought the program was a mere public relations ploy dreamed up in an election year.

The skepticism may well have been valid at the time. The program may have been either or both of those things or, as I believe, it may have been what it appeared to be – a reasonably sincere effort intended to accomplish a national goal – to gain recognition of the basic importance of the teacher in American life. I know that's how Christa saw it and I know that's the opportunity that Christa sought to exploit. But I think that you'll agree with me that how it was conceived is unimportant. What it became is what matters.

It's been so interesting that from the beginning of her selection, all of the articles, especially in New Hampshire but even nationally, suggested that Christa was somehow Pollyanna in teacher's clothing – the girl next door. And actually she was. But she was the best kind of Pollyanna. I think she was a Pollyanna with a strong sense of realism and pragmatism – and – not least important – of politics. Dreams and ideals are wonderful, but if you can't carry them into action you might as well not have them. The important thing is to bring them to fruition and to base accomplishments on your ideals and your dreams . . .

Christa was the most selfless person I ever met, and I don't know anyone who knew Christa who wouldn't say the same thing. She understood and appreciated every moment of her experience that she served in a representative capacity . . . She was not chosen because she was the best teacher or the best spokesman or the best communicator. She was chosen because her talents happened to fit NASA's criteria at that particular time. But she also understood and appreciated at every moment that her mission was to do everything she could to give education a worthy personification . . . A personification that would be effectively heard when she spoke of the critical needs for adequate educational resources – in the national interest. When she demanded salaries to keep the best and brightest in the classroom – in the national interest. A personification who would be ignored by legislators and governors and presidents at their peril. Someone who would be heard by voters, the ultimate authority in our democracy.

I hope you will return to your states and use Christa's efforts and her spirit to get involved in the political arena effectively. To recruit and elect education candidates. To unseat those who support education with their words, but not with their appropriations. And, most of all, that you stay in education until we have a system that honors teachers and rewards teachers as they deserve. Only then will we have the best educational system in the world, and only then will we have the brightest future.

Tributes Begin

In the spring of 1986, seven trees for the seven *Challenger* astronauts were planted in White Park, a short distance from the McAuliffe home in Concord. Caroline and I walked down the hill to attend the ceremony where city officials, friends, neighbors and schoolchildren gathered around Christa's tree. Speeches were made and children took turns shoveling loosened earth around the slight trunk.

We met the dignitaries, pictures were taken, we spoke to reporters and friends, and then we started walking out of the park to go back home. Mary Ruedig, Christa's friend and colleague, fell into step with us.

"I want to tell you," said Mary, "about an elementary school that is being built in Lenexa, Kansas, and named after Christa. My dad is very involved in school affairs there; in fact, he used to be on the Shawnee Mission School Board, and I'm a graduate of Shawnee Mission High School. This may be too soon for you, but I've been asked if you and Mr. Corrigan would attend the dedication."

I was grateful, but Mary was right. There was still too much to absorb. "Mary, thank you for the invitation, and as you understand, I can't think about it as yet. Are you going?"

"Absolutely! Everyone back home is very excited about the new school. They would be so pleased if you could be at the dedication."

This was the best sort of memorial, and I told her gratefully, "If we are unable to make it, it will be nice to know that you will be there to represent Christa."

Later, Ed and I realized that this was something Christa would like us to do. We traveled with Mary to Kansas City, where we were met by her parents, Jean and Walter Hiersteiner. We toured the city, and met officials and the school board. We were taken through the beautiful new school, sat in on some of the classes, and met wonderfully enthusiastic and excited children and teachers.

Jo-Anne Grote, the principal, was justifiably proud. "The children can relate to this school being named Christa McAuliffe Elementary School; they understand, and they're very excited." The school's unique architectural design has classrooms and support services grouped neatly in hexagonal pods surrounding a centrally located administrative and library area. The gymnasium is adjacent and multipurpose; it can be cafeteria and auditorium also.

Dr. Raj Chopra, Shawnee Mission School superintendent, quoted from another portion of Steve McAuliffe's address at the 1986 NEA annual convention: "If you sit on the sidelines, reflect back on Christa as a hero, or a glorious representative, or a canonized saint, rather than putting your energies in accomplishing for her what she wanted to do, then I think her efforts will have been in vain."

Dr. Chopra continued: "We heard him in Shawnee Mission. The board of education proposed that the district's new school be named in honor of this steadfast believer in education. With this gesture, we want to say to the nation, and to education everywhere, that Christa's efforts were not in vain." Following the ceremony there was a balloon release from the playground. Inserted in the balloons were papers on which the students had written their hopes for the future of humankind.

On September 27, 1987, we gathered for the Sunday dedication of the school, which was a festive day with over two thousand in attendance. Mary Ruedig said, "I think Christa would be awed with this beautiful new school, pleased and embarrassed at this lovely dedication."

And we meant our message to the school community: "May your school always be filled with caring and enthusiastic teachers, parents taking an active interest, and children enjoying learning. To honor Christa, you honor all great teachers."

Tributes from New Hampshire

In Concord, a single bell rang a minute for each of the astronauts. A crowd assembled in front of the State House to hear Governor John Sununu say: "Together we watched that journey begin and together we moved from the thrill of success to the grief and shock of sudden disaster. As a nation, we mourn the crew of *Challenger;* as a State we are overwhelmed by the tragic loss of Christa McAuliffe and her mates; and as friends we extend our sympathy and our love to Steve and Scott and Caroline and her parents." Governor Sununu translated his words into action by setting up a Christa McAuliffe Sabbatical Fund controlled by a board of trustees. At Steve's suggestion, the governor asked me to be the family member on the board. On February 21, 1986, the New Hampshire Christa McAuliffe Sabbatical Trust Fund Board of Trustees met for the first time in the governor's office. Contributions had already come in, and fundraising was starting in earnest.

Marilyn Monahan, as president of the local National Education Association, was also a member. (Marilyn has since been elected National Education Association secretary-treasurer and has moved to Washington.) The trustee meetings gave us an opportunity to get together and catch up on a friendship that began when Christa first introduced us. Besides the governor, Marilyn, and me, the board is composed of the president of the state senate, the Speaker of the New Hampshire house, the chair of the State Board of Education, and the state AFL-CIO Teacher Union president.

We devised an application, a shorter version of the one that Christa had filled out for NASA's Teacher-in-Space program, and planned to award the first sabbatical for the 1986–87 school year. That spring, forty public school teachers from every part of the state competed for the Sabbatical Award. As a board, we processed each application selecting finalists, and then after interviewing each one, a final choice was made. Each year the decision has been difficult. It is always a struggle to eliminate so many highly qualified candidates. Marilyn whispered to me one day when we were all trying to reach a decision, "Bet you are wishing as I am that we could see a Christa pop out and make the selection easy!"

The Christa McAuliffe Sabbatical Trust Fund is designed to promote excellence in the New Hampshire educational system, and does so through a fully paid, ten-month sabbatical providing teachers the release time to develop special skills and knowledge, which they later share with school systems statewide. Each year teachers from all over the state apply with a proposal for a program of research, the results of which will be integrated into the curriculum in school districts throughout New Hampshire.

One day after a meeting, Governor Sununu asked me to stay for a few minutes to discuss methods of fund-raising. "What do you think about having a 'Governor's Ski Invitational'? It would not only be fun but I would invite all the governors and ask corporations for sponsorships. A planetarium has been also discussed as a memorial. Would you run these ideas by Steve?"

The ski invitational as fund-raiser sounded great to me – Christa loved to ski, and it would be good source of funds for the teacher scholarships; and I thought Christa would be pleased to have a planetarium in Concord.

The first ski invitational was held in 1988 at Waterville Valley in the New Hampshire White Mountain National Forest. It has become a highlight of the ski season, as a recreational ski race involving mixed teams made up of political figures, Olympic skiers and those just off the beginner slopes, TV and sports personalities, and business leaders.

I am still on the beginner slope. Each year I take a lesson or two. If and when I am able to spend more time learning to ski, I would like to take part in the race. When the instructor took me out for my lesson, he said, "Follow me," and I did – down the slight slope, plowing right into him and landing with the skis up and me down in the snow.

"Still want to take me on?" I challenged the surprised instructor. He was game, and after an hour of instruction I was tired but felt that I'd made some progress.

I went over to the tent and watched the racers come down. When Caroline finished her run, she came over to stand with me.

"How did you do, Grandma?"

"Oh, not too badly, Caroline. Maybe with a lot more practice I'll become a skier."

"Good. Then let's go up and practice. We can ski down together."

"Are you kidding? You want me to try and ski down the side of this hill? The TV cameras will have a field day with me falling all over the place."

"Come on, Grandma, you can do it!"

155

"No way."

"Grandma, you're chicken."

"Caroline, you're right!"

Tributes in Massachusetts

On March 12, 1986, "A Tribute to S. Christa Corrigan McAuliffe" was held in the House Chamber of the Massachusetts State House. Ed drove in from Framingham. Steve and I came from Concord.

Our friend and State Representative Barbara E. Gray presided. Bishop Lawrence J. Riley gave the invocation. Governor Dukakis, House Speaker George Keverian, and Senate President William Bulger spoke. Personal reflections and scholarship tributes were made. Music selections were presented by Framingham State College Chorale and Beaver Country Day School. Massachusetts Teacher-in-Space finalists and Christa's college and high school were all represented. I could see a delegation from the junior high school where I had been substitute teaching just before leaving for the launch in Florida. We were presented with resolutions commemorating the Christa McAuliffe Teacher Incentive Program; the students presented us with flowers.

As we sat and listened, my eyes kept filling up. Then to my horror my nose began to run. Tears will dry on your face, but what can you do about a runny nose? I waited as long as I possibly could and then began to reach for my handkerchief.

Steve nudged me. "If you take that out, you know what is going to happen."

"I have to; my nose is running," I whispered; discreetly as I could, I put my handkerchief to my nose and immediately flashbulbs went off from the back of the room.

"Told you," from Steve.

Of all the pictures taken, of course those were the ones in the newspapers.

The Challenger Center

The Challenger Center was founded by the spouses of the *Challenger* crew to establish a living memorial that would continue the crew's edu-

156

cational mission. The spouses' goal is to establish at least one Challenger Learning Center in all fifty states and many more around the world. Each learning center is composed of two rooms equipped with computer hardware and software. One room is a simulated space station and the other, mission control. Students and teachers work in teams to solve real-life problems during a space-flight simulation. Each mission lasts approximately forty-five minutes, and then the groups change places so that each can have an opportunity to be both on the spacecraft and in mission control. For a successful mission, each team must complete its tasks, working with its practice team. Students and teachers become involved and excited, and that excitement continues after the mission and into the classroom.

One day I received a telephone call from the Challenger Center: "Would you and your husband be interested in traveling to Jordan?"

"Jordan? As in the country?"

"Yes, they are interested in the Center and have invited a delegation to come to discuss the possibilities of their involvement. Steve McAuliffe is unable to go and suggested you since your father's roots are in Lebanon."

Later, landing in Amman, Jordan's capital, we were greeted by the Secretary General of Higher Education and members of his department. We began a full round of interviews, lectures, and presentations, some at schools and universities. Ed and I spoke of Christa's excitement about seeing the world without boundaries, and how she wanted to relay that message to children all over the globe. At the American Community School, teachers stood in line to greet us and tell us how proud they were of Christa.

King Hussein had been out of the country, so much was awaiting his attention. We were told that he wanted to see us and would send word when he was free. We waited all afternoon and early evening, getting tired and hungry. Finally we concluded that the King was probably much too busy for us so we went into the hotel restaurant and ordered dinner.

An array of appetizers had just been placed before us when we were summoned to the palace.

"We haven't eaten!"

"Our dinner is ordered!"

"We're tired, hungry and look crummy."

"How can we meet a king this way?"

"Let's not go!"

At that Lorna Onizuka quipped, "I think we'd better go. He might say, 'Off with their heads!'"

We laughed and left the table, stopping at the restrooms to check if we were presentable.

King Hussein was charming and compassionate. He shook hands with us, apologizing for the long delay. He spoke of the respect that he and his country held for the *Challenger* crew, and extended his sympathy.

After an audience of twenty minutes we followed the King down the hall, and as we left the palace he spoke to each of us and then offered his helicopter for us to travel to Petra and Aqaba the next day.

On the way home from Jordan, we stopped in Vienna to speak to the managing director of the Austrian Solar and Space Agency. He had recently met Barbara Morgan and was interested in the program that the Challenger Center offered.

Relationships between the countries were established. The Challenger Center was making an impact.

A Carillon for St. Jeremiah's

On January 28, 1986, church bells tolled throughout Framingham out of respect for the *Challenger* astronauts. Our pastor, Father O'Connor, received a call and was asked if the parish church bells were ringing. He had to confess that we did not have any bells.

That evening, St. Jeremiah's was overflowing with people stunned by the loss of seven valiant people, one of whom many knew personally. The rectory phone rang incessantly with calls from far and near from those wanting to do something to stem the grief of this loss. At a parish council meeting, it was voted to establish a Christa Corrigan McAuliffe Fund in order to erect a carillon. The announcement in our church bulletin read:

It is hoped that contributions of parishioners, neighbors, and friends will be sufficient to purchase and erect a carillon in the church that would ring out gracing the neighborhood that she once graced with her presence, calling people to worship and pealing hymns of praise each day.

Christa was a member of St. Jeremiah's Parish from its inception, received her confirmation, and was married in this church. During this time, she not only worshipped here and attended the religious education programs, but she was also involved in many parish activities, especially the Girl Scout program. She is well remembered as the star pitcher of the St. Jeremiah Championship Girls Softball Team. Her parents, Edward and Grace Corrigan, are active parishioners with her mother presently a member of the Parish Council and President of the St. Vincent DePaul Society. The ringing of bells would be a reminder to all who hear their peal of the beauty of a young, generous, vibrant lady whose beautiful life sang a song by reaching out.

The blessing and dedication of the Christa Corrigan McAuliffe Carillon took place at a special celebration on Sunday, January 4, 1987. Ed and I had the privilege of ringing the bells for the first time. Ed requested that the first song played be "Amazing Grace."

The bells chime morning, noon, and evening. We can hear Christa's bells at our house. Father O'Connor was delighted to receive a letter that said: "I sit at my desk and at twelve o'clock wonderful music comes in through the open windows. For those of us who work for the school department, may I take this opportunity to say thank you for lifting our spirits every day with the church bells."

A brass plaque set in the bricks outside in the church entrance reads, "The Carillon Bells Are Given in Loving Memory of Christa Corrigan McAuliffe by Family and Friends 1986."

Tributes to Christa as Teacher

In September of 1986 we received a letter from Christa's former colleagues Patricia Mangum and Donna Decker Thompson of Bowie, Maryland:

We are writing to let you know about a project we've been working on here at Thomas Johnson Middle School. We're building a showcase for the front lobby area as a memorial to our Christa. Inside will be various NASA display pieces, photos, items representative of her years in teaching here. We're also installing a bronze memorial plaque outside room 227, Christa's classroom.

We plan to dedicate these gifts to the school in an evening ceremony on Friday November 21, 1986, in conjunction with American Education Week. Guests will be Christa's fellow teachers and friends here and her former students. We think of you often; perhaps our prayers from afar have helped. In reminiscing these last months, we've remembered so many times the pride and love Christa showed when she spoke of you to us.

That November, Ed and I attended the "Friends of Christa" dedication at Thomas Johnson, the school at which Christa taught from 1972 to 1978; there she acquired the experience and developed the judgment that would eventually bring her to selection as Teacher in Space.

Linda Long, Christa's former public relations official, met us at the airport, and we drove to her home in Virginia. Linda's parents were visiting from their home in Delaware. We were all going to the dedication. Bill Green and Bruce Gentile, two of Christa's former students, were picking us up; they were now working for the Prince Georges County Police Department and had volunteered their services.

We had been asked to speak, and I had spent my travel time jotting down the thoughts that I wanted to share. Linda had just had a new computer installed, so we entered my notes into it – and then could not get it to print! I had to hurry and write out my speech in longhand from the computer screen while our drivers waited.

The evening provided us with the opportunity to spend some time with many of Christa's friends, some of whom we knew and others whom we would meet for the first time. Pat Mangum, Donna Decker Thompson, and Carol Sharkey were close friends of Christa's, and the master of ceremonies was Tom Campion, a former colleague of Christa's and a staff member at Thomas Johnson.

Steny Hoyer, a member of Congress from Maryland's fifth district, spoke of knowing Christa from the time that Steve worked as a clerk in his law office in District Heights. Hoyer was then a member of the Maryland State Senate, and Steve was a student at Georgetown Law School. Christa had brought her classes to the law office several times on her famous field trips. Congressman Hoyer said:

> I had the pleasure of seeing her in her role as an enthusiastic and effective teacher. She stopped by my office when she was in Washington on the day before the Teacher-in-Space announcement. She was so excited about what might be ahead of her. After her selection, Christa embraced her duties with great enthusiasm and energy. She became a darling of the press for her naturalness and her ability to encapsulate her mission in just a few profound words.

He also noted that he was no stranger to our town of Framingham, where he had relatives. When it came my turn to speak, I reminded Congressman Hoyer that we also had another tie. His uncle, Dr. Edward Slade, was our dog Jessie's veterinarian!

I remembered that I was first introduced to Thomas Johnson Middle School when I accompanied Christa to school one morning early in her career. We stood outside the classroom as she greeted her students when they arrived. I was not prepared for the size of the young people. They all seemed so huge, and there were so many of them. How could she handle all these kids? She was so young herself and had so little experience. Her room was a maze of posters and projects, a beehive of activity. I was quite relieved and impressed to see that she was very much in control. In retrospect, I realize that Christa's life had been one challenge after another, and this was what she was most comfortable with – meeting challenges.

Discipline and poor attendance were problems, and these she handled by calling the parents of the delinquent student. If that didn't correct the situation, she had the parent come in for a conference. Together they would try to straighten out the problem. One father felt that his whole family was affected by his inability to find work. His English was poor, and he had problems trying to fill out an application. Christa made a bargain with him. "If you come to class after regular school hours, I will teach you enough English so that you can complete an application, *if* you will make sure your son comes to class and does his homework." Each day, the father showed up for his lessons, and when he had gained enough skill and confidence, he applied for and was offered a job. The arrangement had worked.

Gary Kramer, a former student, spoke about living tomorrow today, and about how Christa tried to instill in each of her students the need to be aware of and to understand what was happening in their world:

One way Mrs. McAuliffe widened our scope of reality was to get her classes involved in a project to help build a school in Africa. In this project, the Peace Corps Partnership Schools Program, a village in Africa (in this case, Diolar, Liberia) would raise two-fifths of the money and provide the labor to build a school. The partner school in the United States would provide three-fifths of the funds. Through a bake sale, a newspaper drive, a faculty talent show, and the raffle of a donated $500 television, the students reached their goal of $1,500. All this would not have happened had Mrs. McAuliffe not initiated this outreach. She dedicated herself to teaching young people the art of living well. She taught us, her students, to have a larger vision of our world.

Roger Chapan then spoke. He was in Christa's ninth-grade class during the 1975 school year. Christa was then twenty-six years old – Roger's age now.

It would have sounded ludicrous if anyone had suggested back then that in eleven years she would be a doomed passenger on a space shuttle flight. From my year at Thomas Johnson, the only thing I have saved is a notebook from Mrs. McAuliffe's class. Why? I don't know, but I am now truly glad that I did. It is a notebook from the third quarter. On the title page there are two A+ marks: one for the notebook and one for the third quarter. Beside one of the marks is written, "Good job."

Roger had the notebook with him, and he leafed through it, showing that it was rather thick and that it contained comments from Christa throughout. He commented on the time and effort that she spent on his one notebook; multiply that by thirty in a class, and then by how many classes? "If anything good comes out of this tragedy," he commented, "I hope it is a renewed respect for teachers." Roger recalled

an especially fond memory of a friendly argument I had with Mrs. McAuliffe over a particular quiz. On one question we were asked to explain the acronym ERA. That was new to me, and I was completely stumped. Never one to leave blanks on tests (who knows, you might get lucky), I thought a moment and wrote "Egyptian Republican Army." When grading the paper, Mrs. McAuliffe wrote in the margin "Good try" along with minus 20 points. When I got the graded quiz, I protested vehemently, arguing that she gave initials but didn't cite any clues. She appreciated my zeal, but put me in my place by asking if the "Egyptian Republican Army" had been in the news lately. I couldn't claim that it had, and she pointed out, with a triumphant smile, that this was a current events quiz.

Now my teacher is part of a terrible current event. No one thought back then that it could be such a small and yet sad world.

Christa McAuliffe is remembered for saying, "I teach; I touch the future!" It reminds me of what Plato wrote in the Republic: "Those having torches will pass them on to others." With awe and humility I realize that I am a part of that future Mrs. McAuliffe was referring to. I hope, maybe, that I can carry the torch part of the way.

Carol Sharkey spoke about a library book donation program that would help keep Christa's dream alive. In donated books would appear a bookplate saying that the book was donated by friends of Christa McAuliffe; the program was off to a good start in Colorado, Florida, North Carolina, and many Maryland cities.

Cindy Schott called Christa a team player, both with her students and with the rest of the faculty. She said she felt that Christa would approve of being remembered that way. "Her success was greater when we all shone, not when she shined alone."

In a collection of memories prepared by Christa's students at Thomas Johnson, we read:

Dear Mrs. McAuliffe, We did learn. We learned about bravery and dedication. We learned that a desire to help others can be put ahead of personal comfort and safety. We learned that life can be tragic and shocking. But we also learned that through tragedy we come together as a community, pause and mourn together, and renew our faith to go ahead together. We did learn. Thank you.

Susan Olsen said, in part, "As we grow older, we come to realize that we are also teachers and we share what we have learned from those who most inspired us. The cycle is unending."

Dick Shaner remembered how Christa made him feel about himself. She was a teacher who believed in him, and for this belief, "I owe her thanks."

Other students remembered crocheting a baby blanket together and giving Christa a baby shower before the schoolyear ended. She kept in touch with them, sending baby pictures of Scott and Christmas cards. She was remembered for speaking about college and encouraging them to attend, not only for careers, but for the experience. She spoke to them as a friend.

Wrote one student:

My first memory of Mrs. McAuliffe is her distinct voice. She explained that she was from New England and that's why she had an accent. We never considered the fact that maybe *we* had an accent. Regardless, we always had fun in class talking with our finest Boston dialect (caah = car; yahd = yard). She also told us it was a little difficult for her to talk. She had this new retainer and she felt like she had a mouth full of caramel.

Another commented:

Mrs. McAuliffe related to us as people and had a down-to-earth, honest level of communication with us as students. After an orthodontist appointment, she sympathized with all of us wearing braces because hers were too tight and killing her. We could relate to *this* teacher.

Her students gave her advice on what not to do and what to do concerning braces. She had close rapport with her students. "We knew her limit and the class was always orderly. She was a friend who just happened to be a teacher, too."

When Christa told her classes that she would be moving to New Hampshire, all six classes threw her a surprise party. She was really sorry to be leaving them, but since she and Scott had been living out of a suitcase with friends in Bowie for the past month, she was anxious to join her husband in Concord.

Those on the newspaper staff remember how Christa persuaded the administration to let them personalize the newspaper office by painting it with the school insignia – the roadrunner – on one wall and doing "their thing" on the other three walls. She took them to a building supply store to purchase painting supplies, gave them a sense of ownership, and never went heavy on her editing functions. They called her a "trench worker," typing and mimeographing hundreds of copies on her own time. She was accessible and involved.

"She continued to challenge each of us to say 'yes' to the opportunities of life that come our way," wrote another student, "so we could look back and say 'I did' rather than 'I should have.' For this I thank her immensely."

Kevin Boles wrote:

I missed many of her classes for outside activities, and she supported my work outside of class, as long as I finished my work for her. Often she was not happy with the amount of time I spent on Social Studies, but she tried hard to keep me interested, putting forth individual attention that I didn't expect from most teachers. She sincerely liked her job. She saw it as a personal failure on her part if a student lost interest or was doing badly, and I remember her concern when I did.

Teri Warnick was impressed with the way in which Christa handled her fame during and after the selection process. She quoted Henry David Thoreau, "If one advances confidently in the direction of his dreams and endeavors to live the life which he has imagined, he will meet with success."

Joanne Christoff, one of the students bused to Thomas Johnson to achieve desegregation countywide, indicated that she really didn't feel like part of the school, but she got to know Christa pretty well. "She was easy to get along with and treated all her students kindly. I remember distinctly the poster of the kitten hanging off a limb she had on the wall. It read 'Hang in there, Friday's coming!' That was how I felt. Every day, when I saw that poster, I knew I was in the right place!"

Tim Wilson said that Christa made an impact on his life by helping him decide to attend college, something that he had never considered before her class.

Jan Jensen-Butler wrote that Christa was:

the only teacher who ever *made* me watch television! We analyzed commercials for context, audience orientation, length, and so on. We watched game shows and soap operas so we could see the commercials. It was all related to what we were doing, but it was fun, too. How could we ever imagine that this teacher who we liked so much would turn the country upside-down eight years later.

There were many familiar faces in the audience at the dedication at Thomas Johnson Middle School. We saw Dr. James Lyons, president of Bowie State College, where Christa completed her master's program. We had met Dr. Lyons and his wife and son recently at Framingham State College. Dr. Lyons presented Steve McAuliffe with an honorary doctorate for Christa from Bowie State College, as none of us had been able to be in Maryland to receive it during their commencement. David Zahren, a Maryland finalist for the Teacher-in-Space program, was there, and there were other familiar faces, Christa's friends, and children of her friends. We renewed acquaintances and met other teachers and friends, all with their own stories to tell, and all with tears in their eyes and some weeping openly.

There were many stories to laugh about, too:

Christa, visiting a friend one day, lamented, "I really don't know what I'm going to do about the dishes."

"Why?"

"Well, everything we have has been used and dishes are in the sink or stacked around the sink – maybe we could go to paper plates?"

"But why don't you just wash them?"

"Oh, it isn't my turn."

The next time they were together, Christa's friend couldn't wait to find out how the dishes incident turned out.

"Fine. Steve did them. He just figured he'd wait and do them all at once."

Another time a friend was having a baby and asked Christa's advice about cloth diapers or paper ones. She wanted paper, but her husband thought they should use the cloth. "Well, that's easy," Christa said. "Who is going to wash the diapers?"

The Girl Scouts presented the colors and flag salute at the beginning of the ceremony, and they closed the program with a recessional and retiring of the colors. During the reception, I had the opportunity to speak to many of them. They were excited to know that Christa and I were lifelong Girl Scouts and to learn how much the program meant to us. We admired the museum case, toured the building, and were taken to Christa's former classroom, where her NASA pictures and news clippings were displayed.

Everyone at the dedication was anxious to share their experiences, and we thoroughly enjoyed speaking to all who made the evening such a success and were so much a part of Christa's life.

Our chauffeurs were waiting. We had missed dinner, and it was getting on toward ten o'clock. Bruce and Bill rose to the occasion (after all, they were Christa's students!). They pulled up in front of a lovely restaurant, went in, and explained the situation. They came back saying that we were welcome, the kitchen would be kept open, and a quiet section was being readied for us. We were hungry and tired. Relaxing with good company and fine food was a wonderful way to end our long and emotional day.

Holliston High School

Christa had been scheduled for postflight appearances all over the country; NASA, of course, wanted publicity for their program, and Christa supported that, as she had come to believe wholeheartedly in the possibilities of space research and exploration. But Christa was always her own woman, and she welcomed the rapidly growing schedule as a means of spreading her own message – the importance of support for education, and particularly for the classroom teacher.

We soon realized that we could carry out part of Christa's program for her; that we could foster Christa's message through standing in for her at some speaking engagements. When I was asked by my friends Fosco and Marge Picchi if I would consider speaking at nearby Holliston High School at the annual award banquet on May 13, 1987, I accepted, as I was pleased to pay tribute to the students who excelled in academics, and to their teachers and parents, who shared in that success.

Holliston High School also had special meaning for me since it was there that I did my student teaching in the art department in the spring of 1978. Fosco and Marge taught art classes at Holliston High, and under their skilled and pleasant direction I gained my teaching experience.

I spoke that evening about Christa's training and what she had hoped to accomplish. I spoke of how very privileged we all are and what society expects from us:

> Be true to yourself. Know who you are and who you want to be. Then work at it. Do the tough things. Go out on a rainy winter night and buy that birthday card for a casual friend and mail it, as Christa did. Of course, it's a pain, but as Christa proved over and over to those who knew her, those little things are the most difficult but the most valued tests of our humanity. Those little things are the stuff of successful lives. It is not shuttle flights, or walking on the moon, or being elected president, it is meeting the constant everyday challenges of caring, and of effort, that make us heros. Christa knew that, too, and she was a hero in the only meaningful way – the ordinary way that necessarily blossoms into greatness.

Back to Maryland

Christa McAuliffe Elementary School in Germantown, Maryland, was to be dedicated on April 16, 1988, and the day before, not very far away, a sculpture was to be dedicated in Christa's memory at Bowie New Town Center, near the university, where Christa had received her master's degree. Ed and I decided to attend both dedications.

At the Germantown celebration they did celebrate – all day and evening. We were warmly received and were very impressed with the positive and enthusiastic attitude of everyone we met. We were welcomed with cheers in each classroom. Teachers told us of their pride in their school's name and how they enjoyed informing other educators where they were from when attending county and state meetings.

The McAuliffe school flag was introduced at an outdoor ceremony, and the significance of the design explained. The flag depicts the *Challenger* in space with seven stars and the earth. After the flag was raised, the school song was sung. The children had designed the flag and written the song. As the song ended, red, white, and blue balloons were released, and the children shouted for joy.

We left Maryland overwhelmed by two full days of being with those who had such love and pride for our daughter. How *would* Christa feel?

Efforts to Perpetuate Christa's Work

From around the nation and the world we heard from people who wanted to establish ongoing memorials to Christa; sometimes people we had known were involved, but more often they were strangers who had been captured by Christa's enthusiasm and message.

Ed and I are both graduates of Crosby High School in Waterbury, Connecticut, Ed in 1940 and I in 1941. We received this letter from Ed's class committee:

> The members of the Class of 1940 wish to perpetuate the memory and qualities of Christa McAuliffe. We have established an annual award to go to a Crosby High School female graduating senior who intends to enter the teaching profession and best typifies the spirit and dedication of Christa.
>
> We refer to ourselves as the best ever class to graduate from Crosby. Now

we have the opportunity to prove ourselves correct. We feel we can best express our sympathy to Ed and Grace by establishing this award in their daughter's memory.

Our former neighbor and friend Mary Alice Patterson had moved to Florida, and she and her daughter Marietta were at the launch with us. As thirteen-year-olds, Christa and Marietta ran a neighborhood play school during the summer to make some money for their tuition at Marian High School. Mary Alice was now a member of an American Legion Auxiliary, and wrote to tell us of an annual Teacher-in-Space memorial scholarship that the group had established.

Wrote Gregg and Chris Wright from Nebraska:

You have every reason to be proud of Christa, both for her teaching excellence and for her courage. Her death affected us deeply as it has so many people all over the world.

We believe, like Christa, that supporting teachers is one of the most important things we can do for our future and for our children's future. And we do believe that despite her tragic death, she will have accomplished many of her goals.

To help insure that, we have established a fund which will provide for an annual award to be given to a Nebraska schoolteacher to recognize both excellence and courage in teaching – the Christa McAuliffe prize. This will be administered by the University of Nebraska Foundation, and the selection process will be developed in conjunction with the Teachers' College at the University.

None of us knows why the world works the way it does, but it is certain that it works better for all of us because of the courage and selflessness of people like Christa.

On the fourth anniversary of the disaster, teachers and children from around the Soviet Union gathered at the mission control center near Moscow. The cosmonauts carried a picture of Christa, and they honored her by fulfilling her dream of broadcasting lessons from space.

"This lesson is like passing the torch from the American school teacher to the Soviet cosmonauts," said the mission control director for the Mir Space Station. In a television transmission coming from thousands of miles above the earth, the Mir station commander announced the beginning of a series of lessons. Discussed were new spacesuits being developed for space walks and Soviet life-support systems. From the space station they answered questions from the student audience, and they showed how a Mir laboratory allowed unique crystals to grow.

All five of the Soviet space lessons sent so far have been recorded on videocassette and have been sent to Russian and American schools, as well as to schoolchildren in other countries.

Camp Wabasso

The Infirmary Building – our former Lodge – at Camp Wabasso in Bradford, New Hampshire, was in poor condition, but it held so many wonderful memories that we enjoyed just being there. It was a charming little house with a kitchen to the right of the entryway. On the left was a bath and small library. A living/dining room with enclosed porch ran the length of the house. There was a large fieldstone fireplace, and upstairs there were three large sleeping rooms that could accommodate two, four, and ten, respectively.

This was our favorite place at the Girl Scout Camp. But its condition had deteriorated over the years. The porch sagged and seemed unsafe; doors and windows stuck. Spiders had to be evicted from a slightly rusty tub before it was usable. Springs had sprung through the upholstery. Everything was old and in need of cleaning, painting, replacing, or repairing. We did replace some pieces. Anne Donovan Malovich was even able to bring up a couch in her station wagon. Bonnie Bain Finnigan contributed a dozen wine glasses. We brought up dishes, utensils, tablecloths, candles, and flowers.

The fireplace was fine as long as it had a roaring blaze going. When it died down, the smoke backed into the room and up the stairs, setting off the fire alarm. Many a dash was made up the stairs, followed by frantic pillow-waving to clear the smoke and stop the alarm.

We wanted to bring our meetings at the little house to the Girl Scout Council's attention since we felt that these meetings were noteworthy and might provide Senior Girl Scouts with an incentive to stay with the Scout program. We wanted to return to Girl Scouting a "thank-you" for all that we had been given. We wanted to let others know the value of our friendship. We felt that we had something to share, and we were frustrated because we could not get the council's attention. After discussing possibilities, we decided to do some landscaping around the house by making a "friendship garden." We started by weeding and clearing a space in front of the house beside a large rock that we always used for picture taking. We brought up trowels, shovels, soil, and peat moss. We planted lilies, iris, phlox, and the ground covers sedum, ajuga, and pachysandra. When that was finished, we intended to plant shrubs by the house and put up a small plaque with Troop 315 on it.

Martha Netsch, Director of Communications for Swift Water Girl Scout Council in New Hampshire, had read that Christa drew upon her Girl Scout experiences and skills to help her prepare to take on the challenge of being the first Teacher in Space. Christa had said that the experience that made the greatest single impact on her life was Girl Scouting.

Martha called me in 1985 for an interview, one that I gladly gave. I was delighted that Christa's selection had focused attention on the troop and the friendship that the six women retained. I tried to explain that the bond that joined them was Girl Scouting. I told her about our camping trips and about Gaida Kalnajs, who, as camp director, trained the girls and became their mentor.

I described the training involved when Anne Donovan and Christa were selected to go to the World Wide Senior Round-Up in Farragut, Idaho, in July 1965. For a month before the trip, we hosted a Brazilian girl, Alzira de Souza, who was put in their Round-Up Patrol. (Alzira has remained part of our family and visited us recently with her husband, Sergio Collart.) Bonnie Bain was a Round-Up alternate. As an alternate, she went to a National Girl Scout camping event in Pennsylvania. The next year, our troop sent Joyce Eklund to London, England, where she represented Girl Scouts of the U.S.A. for five months.

For years, the girls "patterned" Patty Kelleher, a girl with cerebral palsy. Working as a team of five, they moved Patty's arms, legs, and head in certain rhythms to stimulate the impaired muscular power. This was done twice a day for half an hour at a time. The troop would take certain days and help out whenever possible.

For six years our troop arranged the program and catered the Inter-Faith Breakfast held on Girl Scout Sunday. They served from 800 to 1,000 girls, parents, siblings, and clergy. One Girl Scout Sunday, it was my birthday. Anne and Christa – who always led the singing – had the crowd render "Happy Birthday" to a surprised and flustered troop leader.

The Framingham *News,* now the Middlesex *News,* always gave the Girl Scouts great coverage, with write-ups and pictures. In 1967, its article on the breakfast ended:

The Senior Scouts of Troop #315 exemplify the highest aims of Girl Scouting in helping to lead and guide others in duty and service to their faith, community, and country. They are participating as leaders and co-leaders to the younger Girl Scouts in the neighborhood troops and are available to all in giving help and service and sharing their knowledge and Girl Scout experience.

I spoke to Martha Netsch for over an hour. I would apologize for going on so, but Martha would urge me on, so I kept talking. This was just the kind of attention that we felt might make a difference to other Girl Scouts and their leaders. Now it would have more clout because the Teacher in Space belonged to our group.

Martha then interviewed Christa and published an article in the January 1986 issue of the Girl Scout regional newsletter, the *Swift Water Current:* "Christa McAuliffe – Teacher, Astronaut, and Girl Scout."

On Sunday, March 9, 1986, Anne Donovan Malavich, Carolyn Bain Bunick, Bonnie Bain Finnigan, Margie Balfour Gilmore, and their daughters attended the Girl Scout Sunday Ecumenical Service held in Framingham by the Midtown Girl Scouts. This service was dedicated to Christa, and a donation was sent in her name to the Edith Macy Training Center in New York.

It was also at this meeting that they met Barbara Donovan, the newly appointed executive director for Patriots' Trail Girl Scout Council. Barbara had just moved to Boston from New York, and spoke of doing something in Christa's name. She initially suggested a "Cape Challenger Ropes Course" that left the women in Troop #315 very unresponsive. In fact, they were feeling a bit dismayed since this was the first time the troop was being given any recognition, and it was only because the *Challenger* explosion had focused attention on them. Since they really didn't expect much of a response, Carolyn spoke up and said, "We would really much rather have the Infirmary building at Camp Wabasso refurbished and used as a friendship house for others as it has been for us."

Our regular camping weekend was coming up Memorial Day, and it would be the first one without Christa. Christa had always done the planning for the meals. Now Anne took over. They invited Lisa to attend, and Lisa accepted, knowing the closeness of Christa's friends would give her comfort, and that she in turn could return that comfort since she was Christa's sister.

I was still up in Concord dealing with the mail, and thought this would be a good time to go home to Framingham. My husband and son were anxious for me to return. Steve and the children were back to all their routines. The mail had been pretty much sorted, answered, and packed away.

On Friday, as I was leaving for the camping weekend, I told Steve that I planned on returning to Massachusetts via Camp Wabasso. But if he should need me for any reason whatsoever, all he had to do was call. "Sure," he said, but I doubted that he really would and said so. He grinned, "We will be okay."

Arrival times always varied, and this weekend we were all together by noon Saturday. We did the usual things, bear hugs in greetings, unloading gear, filling the refrigerator, and claiming a cot for our sleeping bags. But everything was being done at a slower pace, a bit calmer, voices lowered. Discussions would be started, then dropped, for a question would trigger a thought, and we would delve into what really was the central thing on our minds. One person, or sometimes two at a time, would be missing; walks were now being taken for a different reason.

Barbara Donovan had called Anne and asked if she could visit our camp on that Sunday afternoon. She wanted to discuss what we would like the council to do in Christa's memory. Barbara arrived with her sister Agnes, with Cheryle Bartolo, the director of development, and with the makings for Irish coffee. After introductions, we walked around the house and grounds, becoming comfortable with each other. While Barbara and I talked, she asked if perhaps we would like the camp renamed Camp McAuliffe. She laughed when she saw the look on my face as I said, "But that sounds like an army camp!"

"Well, we thought it was a possibility."

I did check with the others, and we were all in agreement that we did not want the name changed – Wabasso had meant too much to too many.

We sat at the picnic table in front of the cottage drinking our coffee and talking. What we really wanted was for the cottage to be repaired and refurnished. Then we were told of plans to demolish the house because it was unsound. Tear down this lovely, charming place that held so many memories?

So we began to speak in earnest, and the Girl Scout officials really did listen. They became aware of the importance that we attached to the house and the significant role that it played in our friendship and how that role could be a role shared with Scouts everywhere.

The questions began, and we started sorting out reasons for and against specific projects. The more we talked, the more it seemed that it just might be possible to save our retreat. We now had something solid to focus upon. A project of substance for Christa, and something we could do ourselves. The weekend was a necessary gathering for all of us, a pulling together, a tightening, a catharsis.

Barbara and Cheryle went back to the Girl Scout office, where they discussed our ideas with the council president. They saw that this project could develop into one of the council's finest resources. They would renovate the Infirmary and turn it into "Christa's House." This would be the initial phase of a much larger project which would include the renovation of the camp dining hall and the establishment of a nature trail to begin at the side of the cottage. In addition, an entire program would be developed for use by as many girls in the council and through-out the country as would like to be part of it. It would be called the Christa McAuliffe Friendship Program.

The Patriots' Trail Board of Directors approved the project and the program, and a volunteer task group was appointed to support the funding of the project.

We were delighted!

Christa's House would be freshly insulated, given new plumbing, electrical work, and windows. To all appearances, it would look just the same, only newer, cleaner, and structurally sound!

The house would be used by former Girl Scouts to hold reunions and for Girl Scout leader renewal meetings. It would also be used by older Girl Scouts in the same way that Troop 315 used it – to forge friendships and keep them alive.

The friendship program was to have a logo, and I requested that there be an apple for the teacher, a sign for friendship, the sky and stars for Christa's motto, and the shuttle which Christa had hoped would bring her to the stars.

Barbara brought two staff members and a board member to our house to discuss the program that they had worked on and to bring us some sketches of the logo so that we could choose one. The logo that we selected included all that I had asked for plus the rocket's plume in rainbow colors to suggest the many interrelationships which are created through friendship. The logo is now on an embroidered patch that signifies completion of the year-long Christa McAuliffe Friendship Program, a program offered to all ages, and one that is goal oriented and challenging.

The dedication of Christa's House and the Nature Trail took place on Sunday, August 7, 1988, marking the completion of the first two phases of the Christa McAuliffe Friendship Center.

The council had arranged for Ed and me to have a suite at the Bradford Inn, not far from the camp, so that we could arrive the day before the ceremony and not have to make the drive on the day of the dedication. The rest of our group was staying in Christa's House, and were the first ones to use it since it had been remodeled.

After we checked in, Ed and I went over to the camp. Even coming up to the house was exciting. A new brick walkway led to a welcome mat at the door. Shrubbery was planted along the front and a box under the kitchen window was filled with flowers. Everything was so neat! "The girls" and Jean Sanborn were waiting for us. With a bit of wonder, I started to explore. Since Ed had never been inside the house, I had to keep explaining my excitement with, "but you should have seen it before!" It was quite a strange feeling to walk through this house, so familiar and yet so different. All the shabby and old had become bright, shiny, and new.

The committee and builders did a fabulous job. Things worked! No spiders in the immaculate tub! You could go out onto the enclosed porch without falling through the floor! You could even open the windows! Everything was sturdy and gleaming, and best of all, everything was still the same. And we had two working bathrooms! Oh, Christa, what you have done!

That evening, we met Betty Pilsbury, National President of Girl Scouts of the U.S.A. Barbara Donovan had arranged for the four of us to have dinner at the Bradford Inn so that we would have a chance to become acquainted.

The next morning, our group met at the house to put together the thoughts that we wanted to share at the ceremony. I was to introduce each speaker after Ed and I presented our gift, Christa's signed official NASA portrait, the new friendship badge, and her Teacher-in-Space patch all framed to hang in the house.

People began arriving. Since regular camp was in session, guests were treated to a water show, horse show, and demonstrations of crafts and skills by the campers. Steve came up with Scott and Caroline for the brunch. Scott had to register for soccer at four o'clock, so Steve and Scott left, but Caroline was able to stay with us.

The bugler sounded assembly, the camp chorus sang, and the colors were presented. The podium was in front of the house, which was flanked by flags, and the speakers sat off to the side. The guests were facing the house, seated on chairs or on the lawn; some were even standing beneath the trees and in the open field.

The council president gave the welcoming address, and the Nature Trail and garden log were presented by Garden in the Woods, an affiliate of the New England Wildflower Society. The Christa McAuliffe Friendship Program logo, worked into a banner, was presented, and two Senior Girl Scouts described the symbols.

Jean Bain Sanborn and I had been privileged to be leaders of Troop 315. Jean presented an attractive wall hanging that she made symbolizing the camp. "As you know," she explained, "Wabasso comes from a local Indian word for *rabbit*. This rabbit is surrounded by Girl Scout memorabilia and was lovingly made to hang in Christa's House."

Margaret Balfour Gilmore gave an overview of their friendship:

To all of us, Scouting means many things, but above all, Scouting means the dedication to excellence and the commitment to friendship. My friendship with Christa began and in a sense ended with Scouting. As members of the same troop, we experienced together the joys of Scouting. We and several other members of our troop remained friends through high school, college, marriage, and children, and we returned for our reunions at Camp Wabasso throughout the years.

To be with us, Christa flew up from Houston where she was in the final stages of her training. She spoke of the excitement of going into space, of her continuing involvement in Scouting, and of her intention to take a Girl Scout pin up with her.

Margie ended by saying:

Christa knew that anything was possible if you put your mind to it and believed, and if you reached for the stars. I always respected and admired her for that and saw her become a fine mother, devoted teacher, and finally an astronaut. For all of us, Christa was a source of inspiration and an example of the embodiment of the spirit of Scouting. All the members of Troop 315 are delighted and very appreciative of the time, effort, and financial support which have made Christa's House possible.

Carolyn Bain Bunick talked about their first reunion in Maine in December 1979 and about why Wabasso had become so important:

For several years, we had lost contact . . . While visiting Joyce's home in Maine, we began to reminisce about our mutual friends in Scouting, and since Christa lived in Concord only a couple of hours away, we called her, singing our typically off-key rendition of "Girl Scouts Together." Christa didn't know who we were at first, but our singing soon gave it away. She had been in touch with others, so we quickly organized a get-together the following day. By the time we had assembled, there were sixteen of us. Six adults and ten children, and four of the children were under six months of age. It was a wonderful day. We caught up on ten years of each other's lives, and we became reacquainted. We talked of returning to Wabasso as a group. Christa volunteered to organize our first camping weekend and did so even to the point of sending us postcards detailing everyone's responsibilities. As we continued to meet here, the years melted away, and we regained our feelings of warmth and belonging.

Anne Donovan Malovich had always been close to Christa, serving as maid of honor when Christa married. As teenagers, they went together to the Round-Up in Idaho, which Anne described as a high point in her Scouting career. "In preparing for Round-Up, we had to do many difficult tasks that we couldn't understand the purpose of, such as pitching a tent blindfolded." Anne also told about going to visit Gaida Kalnajs, their trainer and mentor, who was at the Round-Up:

Gaida was on the opposite side of the huge encampment. We finally located her tent to find that she was out and would return shortly. Christa and I decided to wait for her, not realizing how late it had become. When Gaida finally appeared, she was thrilled to see us, but appalled that it was ten minutes to curfew. We were very far from our campsite. Christa and I set out on the perimeter road, a little nervous about the lateness of the hour. Military police patrolled these roads in a jeep, so every time we heard a motor or saw headlights, we dove into the brush at the side of the road to escape detection. Our luck ran out though, and we were confronted by two stern-looking MPs. They lectured us all the way back to camp. Christa and I were terrified, contemplating the consequences of what we had done. We could picture ourselves being sent home in disgrace from Idaho, and how our fathers would be unhappy with us. Instead, we were simply warned to be more careful and sent on our way. Fortunately, it was our last brush with the law.

Anne went on to talk about the storm that hit camp the day before they were to leave:

The peaceful and sunny afternoon was interrupted by the blare of a sound truck. "Warning," the voice said. "A violent storm is approaching. You have fifteen minutes to break camp." The race was on! In the distance over the mountains, a huge black cloud was closing in on the valley. We quickly struck the tents leaving only the kitchen tarp standing when the storm hit. With two girls hanging on each of the four poles, we managed to keep the tent from blowing away while being buffeted by the wind and drenched by the rain. The storm was over as suddenly as it occurred. But what a mess it left! Because two of the four patrols were scheduled to leave the next day, we were in a terrible bind. We couldn't pack the wet tent. Everything we owned was drenched, and we had nowhere to spend the night. Thirty-two girls quickly organized everything without adult supervision. We managed a place to sleep, food was shared, chores and tasks assigned, and our problems solved. Our leader, who had been caught in another area when the storm hit, returned to find everything under control. We had done it ourselves. Suddenly all the hours of training and drills made sense. All the skills we had developed over the years of Girl Scouting had been put to use. And I think we can all agree that we have drawn on those skills all our adult lives. For that we thank Girl Scouting.

Bonnie Bain Finnigan stepped up next and spoke about the impact that we had made on the lives of one another:

Once we were back at Camp Wabasso as a troop of adults, we began to reflect on why this coming together was so important. As we looked back on Cadette and Senior troop experiences, we were able to identify some of the qualities that had given us this bond.

Bonnie gave us leaders part of the credit, referring not only to Jean Sanborn, Mary Eklund, and me but also to Jean Bagley and Jay Swanson, who had been their leaders when the girls were Cadettes:

We grew up with leaders who believed in us and in the unlimited scope of our abilities. Our activities included community service projects individually chosen by each member of the troop. We were encouraged and supported in our endeavors by troop members and our leaders.

She spoke about various projects including "patterning" Patty Kelleher and preparing the Girl Scout Sunday breakfast:

This breakfast helped earn us enough money to go to the World's Fair in New York and to help send our Round-Up representatives to Idaho. As time went on, members of our troop left for college. Although it became more difficult to meet regularly, we still made time for Sunday morning breakfast meetings. Our feelings for each other developed into wonderful friendship. During the time most difficult for teenagers, we had the confidence and support of our friends to pull us through. In an atmosphere of respect and concern, we became a group of young women ready to try almost anything. So none of us was particularly surprised when Christa was chosen as Teacher in Space. We knew she could do it. Mrs. Corrigan's words come back again and again. "Try it. You can do it!"

Bonnie then described how Christa had torn herself away from so many other commitments to spend that last night with them at camp in October of 1985, how they had tried to toast her celebrity, and how she stopped them with a cheerful, "No, this toast should be for all of us!" "This was Christa," said Bonnie, "and this is the feeling we all have for each other."

Next spoke Joyce Eklund Knight, who has made Girl Scouting her career. Joyce started by saying:

I'd like to tell you how it happened and where our dream can go. From our first reunion here, we have talked about the unique opportunity we have to go back to our youth, and to have time to reflect what roles Girl Scout values have played in our lives. During our time here at Wabasso, our laughing, crying, working, singing, and (almost) nonstop eating blend to create a wonderful mixture of fun and friendship. We talked frequently about how to make the Infirmary better, how to fix it up, and how to provide the opportunity for others to experience what we have: to fill one's cup with friendship, love, and acceptance; to be a powerful force for good in today's world. Christa has shown that to all of us.

On behalf of Troop 315, I'd like to invite all Girl Scout adults and older girls to share in our dream come true. Come to the Christa McAuliffe Friendship Center, have fun, renew yourselves, strengthen your friendships, and challenge yourselves to be all that you can be."

Our daughter Lisa has joined our group. At first she was there because she was Christa's sister, and now because she is Lisa. Children are always welcome on our long weekends as long as they are too young to walk or talk. Lisa, attending the ceremony with her two-month-old son Michael, commented:

In the spring of 1986, Christa's friends of Troop 315 made their biannual trip to Camp Wabasso, inviting me along. Together we planted flowers in front of what is now Christa's House. We talked, laughed, and cried. We remembered Christa as a daughter, a sister, a friend. There is a Girl Scout song that says it all: "Make new friends but keep the old. One is silver, the other is gold." The Christa McAuliffe Friendship Center is a tribute to the golden relationship among Scouts. Therefore, we would like to present to the house a friendship journal for all who come here. We have made the first entries and hope the women of the future will find that which will serve as a record for all who come here of the fun, happiness, and friendship that we have shared.

The rain was still holding off, but it seemed to be imminent. An announcement was made about where each group of guests should seek shelter if the heavens did open up.

Betty Pilsbury was introduced next. In her speech, she said:

To be an astronaut required applying, taking tests, and undergoing training to demonstrate mental, physical, and emotional suitability. These were hurdles that Christa had already leapt over back in 1965. She was able to join and make friends quickly with the NASA scientists and pilots. I would like to think that this was because of her years of working cooperatively with other Girl Scouts.

Betty spoke of the Friendship Center and ended by saying, "Wouldn't Christa have loved it!"

Finally, the time came for the actual dedication. As the house was dedicated, three generations of Girl Scouts – Caroline, Lisa, and I – unveiled the plaque that is on the front of the house. The plaque reads:

Christa's House
celebrating the memory of teacher-astronaut
Christa McAuliffe
whose love of Girl Scouting inspired this Friendship Center
August 7, 1988

The chorus started singing "Girl Scouts Together," and everyone joined in while twenty white doves were released, dipped their wings to the crowd, and flew away. The sun had just broken through the clouds.

Ed and the Girl Scouts

Ed and I, Anne, Joyce, and Margie were guests at the Patriots' Trail Girl Scout Council's 1987 Annual Meeting on April 30, 1987, at the Copley Plaza in Boston. More than 500 volunteers were celebrating Girl Scouting's seventy-fifth anniversary. I had the opportunity to thank them for making the Christa McAuliffe Friendship Center possible.

That evening we met Girl Scouts and Girl Guides from other parts of the world. We were introduced to a Girl Guide from Lebanon who was in the United States studying to be a doctor. That reminded me of the time so very many years ago when a young doctor from Lebanon, a relative of mine through my uncle Professor Hitti, had dinner with us when we were living in Boston. He was in this country visiting various hospitals before he went back to Beirut, where his father was chief of the hospital. When I mentioned this to the Lebanese Girl Guide, she asked, "Could that be any relation to Dr. Philip Hitti, the historian?" When I said yes, she became excited. "But every school child knows Dr. Hitti! He has written histories of the Arabic countries. We use his books in school!"

The 1989 annual meeting was held in Framingham, and Ed and I were given an award for our support of Girl Scouting. Ed was unable to attend that evening, so my family group consisted of Anne and Margie. Accepting the award, I stressed how supportive and proud Ed was that Christa and I found such pleasure in the Girl Scout program. Having four younger children, he did quite a bit of babysitting and more than his share of driving.

I told them about some of the activities that we shared. The girls in my Senior troop were involved in primitive camping at the Senior Patrol Encampment at Camp Featherfin in Holliston, Massachusetts. Gaida Kalnajs was the camp director, and I was Senior Advisor. Betsy, six, and Lisa, seven, came with me and slept in my tent.

The camp is on Lake Winthrop, and to reach it we had to enter through a cemetery, park the car at the rear of the cemetery, and then carry our gear over a small stone wall and walk up a pathway that led to camp.

Our wedding anniversary happened to be on one of the Saturday nights while we were camping. Christa gave us tickets to see Carol Lawrence in *Funny Girl* playing at the Carousel, an open-air theater in Framingham. I received permission to be away from camp for that evening, so along with my camp jeans and shorts, I packed appropriate clothes so I would be dressed for the theater when Ed came to pick me up.

At the end of the evening, we drove back to camp, through the cemetery, parked the car, and, using a flashlight, made our way over the wall and through the path to my tent. Since I wouldn't be needing my dress any longer, Ed waited for me to change and then put my dress, slip, stockings, and shawl over his arm, held my heels in one hand and the flashlight in the other, and kissed me goodbye.

Leaving my tent, his parting words were, "If I should meet a policeman, he will want to know why I am in a cemetery at midnight carrying women's clothing. And he will probably say, 'Okay, fellow, where's the body?'"

Another evening at the same camp, the girls were given permission to attend a local dance, and we made transportation arrangements. Ed was one of the drivers. We picked the girls up at eleven o'clock to take them back to camp. Our car was the first to drive up to the cemetery. As we approached, we saw a car blocking the entrance – a young couple parking. Ed pulled up and walked over to the car to ask them to please move so he could drive through. Needless to say, they both looked startled as to why anyone would want to drive into a cemetery at night. And when Ed added, "Don't come right back because there are more cars coming," they became frightened, started the car quickly, and raced away from the kind of people who would be holding a meeting in a cemetery at midnight.

So you see, Ed certainly did become involved in our Girl Scout activities!

Educators and Fellows

Donations from across the nation came into the National Education Association in Christa's name. The NEA gave these funds to the National Foundation for the Improvement of Education (NFIE) to establish the Christa McAuliffe Institute for Educational Pioneering. Each year, after a national search, five Christa McAuliffe Educators are selected. From a theme, the Educators develop the plans for a summer conference to be held at Sanford University. Then from a national competition, the NFIE selects Christa McAuliffe Fellows, teams of practicing teachers working in an area related to the theme. These fellows participate in the conference designed by the educators. The theme for the first year's conference was "Preparing All Students for the 21st Century: Creative Uses of Technology in Education."

Ed and I attended the first conference in the summer of 1988. There we met the five educators and twenty fellows, along with the executive director, Donna Rhodes, the project director, and the institute staff. We were delighted to find Peggy Lathlean, one of the ten finalists for the Teacher-in-Space program, there as part of the staff.

We had a wonderful few days getting to know these dedicated teachers and sitting in on some of the work activities. It was rewarding for us to see them in action, all wearing white shirts with blue lettering, with Christa McAuliffe Institute for Educational Pioneering over their hearts and NFIE on their sleeves.

We weren't able to attend the 1989 sessions, but in 1990 I attended the reception held in Washington, D.C., to honor the 1990 educators; that followed the screening of the ABC television movie "Challenger."

I thought that it might be difficult to watch the movie, and it wasn't easy until I realized that Christa was not really being portrayed in the film. That character did not have her depth. The 51L crew were hardworking, dedicated people. Where was that portrayed in the film? This was a bit of fluff.

When I congratulated the five new educators, I looked out into the audience of teachers, principals, and superintendents. Here was the substance not shown in the film. These people were Christa. Here was dedication, professionalism, and desire to make a better future. And there in the audience I saw Judy Garcia. Judy was on the Teacher-in-Space team, and had been romping on the beach with Christa and Barbara Morgan when Linda Long thought they ought to be sleeping. We spent a short hour together after the reception and before my flight home.

The U.S. Department of Education funds a fellowship program for full-time public and private school teachers. Massachusetts Department of Education sponsored a meeting of the 1989 and 1990 Christa McAuliffe Fellows from the six New England states.

Dr. Beverly Weiss, now director of the Christa Corrigan McAuliffe Center at Framingham State College, and I went to the all-day session in Boston. A guard greeted us as we entered the Post Office building and, without asking any questions, gave us directions to the Education Department. As we picked up our purses from the detector belt and walked over to the elevators, we looked at each other and laughed quietly: "Do we ever look like teachers! He knew exactly where we were going!"

When I hear from an Educator or a Fellow, it is a warm feeling to know that Christa's name and spirit are out there in so many wonderful teachers doing wonderful things. Christa was always thrilled when someone would come up to her and say proudly, "Christa, I'm a teacher, too!" I know that feeling.

Memorials and Funding Troubles

After the *Challenger* explosion, the Astronauts Memorial Foundation was conceived by Alan Helman, a local architect, to be a nonprofit corporation committed to broadening our knowledge and understanding of space exploration and dedicated to remembering those United States astronauts who gave their lives in the space program.

In July 1986, the foundation and NASA agreed to establish the astronaut memorial on the grounds of the Kennedy Space Center at Cape Canaveral, Florida. The program would honor those who have perished in the pursuit of space exploration; at this time there were fourteen in all. Four pilots – Charles Bassett, Theodore Freeman, Elliot See, and Clifton Williams – lost their lives in T-38 training accidents, and in 1967, Gus Grissom, Ed White, and Roger Chaffee died in the Apollo I fire. When the *Challenger* exploded in 1986, it took seven lives: Dick Scobee, Mike Smith, Judy Resnick, Ellison Onizuka, Ron McNair, Greg Jarvis, and Christa.

In October 1989, the foundation dedicated the cornerstone of the memorial by having members of each astronaut's family insert a gold star into a large plaque engraved with the words *To Those Who Gave Their Lives to Bring the Stars a Little Closer*. The memorial stands by a lagoon at the Visitors Center Complex. Made of highly polished black granite 40 feet high and 50 feet wide, the astronauts' names have been cut through the granite surface; sunlight caught by glass inserts causes the names to glow. Lighting provides the illumination when there is no sun.

A few days after the dedication of the cornerstone, the foundation was having its third annual recognition dinner. Ed and I stayed on to attend. We relaxed, and I did a little swimming in the outdoor pool.

I'm prone to rashes and could feel one coming on, but I was controlling it with medicated cream. Whether the heat or the chlorine in the pool water triggered the rash, I don't know, but I sure looked a mess the next morning. Looking back from the mirror was a blotchy face, puffed eyes, and red bumps all over my throat and shoulders. The black-tie affair was that evening. I'd sure be a sight in my off-the-shoulder gown! I called the desk and was directed to a walk-in clinic a few blocks away. It was early, and only a few people were waiting. When the nurse called me in, the doctor looked me over. She felt it was an allergic reaction, a combination of heat, water, and stress.

I'm not in the habit of describing myself as Christa's mother, but I told the doctor why it might be stress, explaining why I was in Florida and where I planned to go that evening.

"Well, that's all pretty stressful and certainly adds to the problem, but I think we can get you in better shape for tonight with a cortisone shot." Then she continued, "You know, I can't tell you how much we admire Christa and the tremendous loss that we in Florida feel." She excused herself and returned with two nurses. "We understand that you are Christa's mother. We would like to give you a hug." I got hugs, a shot, and advice: stay out of the sun and the water. Try to stay away from stress!"

I am always touched when people tell me how much Christa means to them. So many people care about me because I am her mother. I think they feel they are hugging her through me. I was sent away from the doctor's office with pills and ointment. The shot did a good job. That evening, my skin still felt rough, but the puffiness was gone. If anyone thought about it, they'd probably figure that I'd been in the sun too long.

In the spring, some of us went to Tallahassee, Florida, to lobby on behalf of the foundation. Funding for the foundation was coming through the sale of commemorative Florida license plates; the state of Florida had already cut fifty percent from the proceeds, and now a bill was introduced in the state legislature to take away the remaining fifty percent. The memorial and its maintenance had been realized, but the second phase, an educational center, had not been started. Revenue from the license plate sales was necessary; the center would cost $14 million. The foundation was expecting $7 million from the *Challenger* license plates, and the rest from corporate donations. The foundation president and the board of directors had been trying to persuade the lawmakers of the foundation's importance.

We spent the day at the Capitol, holding press conferences and lobbying. For whatever reason, the foundation's dedication, our lobbying, or other causes, the bill to withdraw the remaining fifty percent never made it to the floor, so there was no vote. The Astronauts Memorial would receive its share of the license plate proceeds that year.

But the events in Florida did not represent the only occasion when the efforts to honor Christa and the other *Challenger* crew members ran into funding difficulties. A national teacher-training scholarship program was established in Christa's name after the *Challenger* explosion. But funding for the program was eliminated in the federal budget for fiscal 1988 that was submitted by President Reagan in December 1986.

This omission prompted Christa's father to write a letter of protest to the president. "How can you praise Christa and then take away the means of funding a memorial to her?" he asked.

Excuses were made, and Ed was offered assurances that "the president has not forgotten Christa McAuliffe," but obviously someone had. Fortunately, there were supporters of the McAuliffe Scholarship Fund. The fund was reinstated. It was a sad commentary that Christa's father found it necessary to remind President Reagan about his promise.

Christa McAuliffe Planetarium

On June 21, 1990, the Christa McAuliffe Planetarium on the grounds of the New Hampshire Technical Institute in Concord was officially opened. Those attending a forty-five-minute preview sat in reclining seats beneath a forty-foot dome that crackled with light as it journeyed into space.

Louise Wiley, a fifth- and sixth-grade teacher from Pittsfield, provided the idea that resulted in the planetarium construction, with then Governor Sununu supporting state funding. Now that it exists, the planetarium seems an obvious way of honoring the woman who dreamed of teaching in space.

The planetarium is equipped with the most advanced digital planetarium projection system in the world and offers a computer-generated star field, making it possible to see how a sky changes over a span of two million years. It is capable of simulating space travel in three dimensions up to 600 light years from earth. Each seat in the auditorium has a control panel that allows viewers to chart their own journeys through the cosmos.

The planetarium has unprecedented flexibility. Teachers can operate the system themselves and tailor programs for their classes. Students are able to stop shows in midstream to ask questions. When Dr. Robert Brown, director of NASA's Educational Affairs Division, spoke at the groundbreaking in October 1988, he said:

In my mind, this represents a continuation of the national healing process. This project makes the goals behind NASA's Teacher-in-Space program a living, substantial reality. To teach students to think like scientists, they have to learn like scientists. The hands-on approach is best.

At the opening, Dr. Walter Hawley, a science teacher and chairman of the Planetarium Commission, did more than talk. He quickly brightened the cloudy day by taking the crowd through a joyous series of stunts. He had the audience touching their hands overhead saying, "This is the pyramid, the apex, and reaching, as you know Christa reached." He noted that it was appropriate to dedicate the planetarium on the summer solstice.

"To reach is to wonder," he concluded. "Christa was curious and we have to be curious. The glistening pyramid, with blue-glass skin that reflects day and night skies is New Hampshire's living memorial." He led the crowd in a joyful clapping of hands and then holding of hands, getting a ripple of laughter as the audience watched the dignitaries on stage holding hands.

Steve spoke, remembering his wife as a teacher and an extraordinary person. "Christa would surely stand and applaud. Christa would insist that I tell all who are privileged to experience the planetarium programs to read not only her name above the door, but to read also the names of the many exceptional teachers who labor every day for our children's futures." He said of his wife, "She knew she was not uniquely qualified to fly in space. She was selected because she was a teacher. Memorials can inspire," he said, "but this one will do more than that – this one will serve. Christa would be, and I suppose she is, very proud and very pleased."

As the keynote speaker, Admiral Richard Truly, the former astronaut who was brought in to head NASA after the *Challenger* disaster, recognized Christa's entire family from the oldest to the youngest, Lisa's eleven-day-old daughter asleep in her arms. Admiral Truly called the planetarium a schoolhouse, "a place to continue the work Christa believed in. The sky itself is a schoolhouse," he continued, adding that the "planetarium may be the only classroom in America where students will complain that the classes are too short."

Admiral Truly concluded with a tribute to Christa:

Christa was many things, but she was not weak at heart. Your state should be proud of this facility. Christa understood that space could be a catalyst for young people to do better. This planetarium is more than a memorial to Christa McAuliffe, as a matter of fact, it is more than a planetarium. It is a promise to continue the work she believed in and a promise to fulfill her dream.

Eileen O'Hara reflected that Christa, as a social studies teacher, presented an opportunity for her to look at space in a different way. Space, she said, can be a source for painting, writing, history, mythology, music, and math. The planetarium, along with teachers, can show us a new way to look at the night sky. She commented that she would like to see future plans include teacher workshops and construction of classrooms on the site. The potential for learning is terrific; workshops and classrooms would give teachers an opportunity to continue to do what Christa McAuliffe knew was important.

Lisa said, "We miss her so very much, and this is one way to keep her spirit alive."

Kit had been worried that people would forget Christa. "Now I know they will remember, and it's a great feeling," he said.

Me? I'm so very proud of Christa. How she would love to be here!

Christa's Philosophy of Education

Christa ran a classroom based on mutual respect, asking two things of her students: that they be themselves and that they do the best they could. As Christa prepared to be the Teacher in Space, she spoke of her goals and her understanding of her role:

> Any dream can come true if you have the courage to work for it. I would never say, "Well, you're only a C student in English so you'll never be a poet!" You have to dream. We all have to dream. Dreaming is okay.
>
> Imagine me teaching from space, all over the world, touching so many people's lives. That's a teacher's dream! I have a vision of the world as a global village, a world without boundaries. Imagine a history teacher making history!
>
> This is a very exciting time in my life, 36 exciting years behind me, 36 more ahead of me.

Christa also quickly understood that her mission would fail without the press. To excite a nation about education and space she needed to excite reporters first. She quickly adopted them as her students, and her press conferences became classrooms.

As the Teacher in Space, Christa sought to restore respect for teachers and their profession. She described herself as "an ordinary person in extraordinary circumstances." Her mission, as she saw it, was to demystify the space program and share it with other ordinary people.

When asked how teaching the same lessons over and over again could be exciting, Christa would say, "That's what teachers do best. Each time we are reaching new students. For them, it is a new lesson, and we must be able to make it exciting for them."

Ed's Death

Ed died on January 25, 1990. The previous year he had experienced weight loss, and had undergone chemotherapy and radiation. He was drained and tired of trying to fight the cancer. "I don't want to live like this. It's time for me to go. I've had a good, full life with no regrets except that I won't be with you anymore."

"You'll be with Christa."

"Yes."

Father Jim Leary said the Memorial Mass for his cousin on Sunday, January 28, 1990. Steve spoke of his father for all of us: "He was always there for us. He was, most of all, a family man." Steve mentioned that his father always was at school games and then later followed his softball games. "Sometimes he might be detained at the office and arrive late, but I always knew he would come." He spoke of Ed's wry humor and quick wit that could be sharp at times. He spoke of the traits that the children had inherited from him and of the love and pride he had for all his children and grandchildren. "And he was a smart man – he married my mother."

Ed would have been justly pleased with his son's tribute, the Mass, the music, and the church filled with his family and friends.

So another change has taken place in our lives. His sharing and support are no longer here for us.

Completion

While we were in Florida awaiting the shuttle launch, Ceil and Charlie Wohler had a key to our house. They came by to take in the mail and feed and walk Jessie, our part collie, part golden retriever.

On January 28, 1986, the television cameras, the reporters, and the curious came swarming around our house. They were snapping pictures and going up and down the street talking to neighbors.

The Wohlers were kept busy answering the door and telephone. At the beginning, they tried to be polite and answer questions. "But what are they really like?" one reporter asked. Ceil tried to show him our hallway filled with family pictures and some of my paintings on the walls. When she took the card that Christa had sent me from Houston – of a woman mountaineer helping another woman to the top – from the refrigerator door and showed it to him, the newsman just looked disgusted. She then realized that wasn't the story that he wanted to write. Charlie showed him to the door. After that, they let no one else into the house.

On February 5, 1986, we were gathered at home waiting to leave for St. Jeremiah's Church to attend Christa's second memorial funeral Mass. The first one had been in Concord, New Hampshire, two days earlier.

I found Christa's cousin Father James Leary reading the card on the refrigerator.

On May 18, 1986, Father Jim accepted a degree for Christa from St. Joseph's College in West Hartford, Connecticut. He came to Framingham to give us her hood and diploma and said that when he accepted her honorary degree, he spoke about the card that he had read on our refrigerator door. Christa's simple little card had left its impression on him, too. He also quoted from Steve McAuliffe's letter of appreciation to St. Joseph's College for the honorary award for Christa. "She had hoped," Steve wrote, "that her representative role, as she recognized it to be, might inspire students to dream, might draw public attention to the worthy contribution of teachers, and that it might in some small way lend support to the growing efforts of women to achieve equal status and opportunity in our society."

As I finish writing this, Christa, it has been five years since you have gone. Your dad and I have spent a great deal of that time trying to carry out the work you started. The number of people that you have touched is overwhelming. You are in so many hearts and minds.

I am still signing your pictures and speaking to students, teachers, and Girl Scouts. You can't imagine how many teachers are Christa McAuliffe Scholars, Fellows, and Educators! Your legacy is ongoing and gathering strength year by year. Teachers are standing tall and proud of their profession. Students are now trying to reach those goals that they once thought unobtainable. You have made this world a better place.

What you had wished for is finished, Christa – this is your journal.

With love,

Mother